Without a Map

D1600322

Without a Map

· · · · · · ·

A Caregiver's Journey through
the Wilderness of Heart and Mind

LISA STEELE-MALEY

TURNING
STONE
PRESS

Cover design by Frame25 Productions
Cover art by Duncan Steele-Maley
Interior design by Howie Severson/Fortuitous

Turning Stone Press
8301 Broadway St., Suite 219
San Antonio, TX 78209
turningstonepress.com

Library of Congress Control Number
is available upon request.

ISBN 978-1-61852-122-4

10 9 8 7 6 5 4 3 2 1

Printed in the United States of America

*Dedicated to my family
and to the grace that awakens in the
heart of giving and receiving*

Disclaimer

This is my true story. The people and events described here are real, as are the worries, questions, joys, sorrows, and other emotions they evoked.

With respect, I have changed the names of the doctors and the residential living facility to protect professional privacy.

With appreciation, I have used my family members' real names. At different times and in different ways, they offered support, advice, presence, and vital companionship. Their experience of these events will be different from mine; I am grateful for their permission to share my perspective.

Table of Contents

Introduction

Over the course of five years, my father succumbed to progressive dementia. As my family navigated the uncharted territory of supporting him, I was surprised over and over again by how hard the process was and by how much there is yet to understand about dementing illnesses. I scoured the library and the internet for information and guidance. Some of what I read helped to explain what was happening medically and some shed light on what the experience might be like from my dad's perspective. Some resources offered a range of possible conditions that could be causing his dementia and sketched out the likely progression ahead. They were helpful, but they were not enough. I craved clarity and answers. I wanted a map.

I have spent most of my adult life traveling in the wilderness. Although I always carry a map, I never really know exactly what to expect. A map provides landmarks and guideposts that offer comfort and perspective, but a trip carefully planned while consulting the contours and promises of a map will always adapt to a myriad of unknown variables. In this case, there was not even a map—and I definitely did not know what to expect. Dad's situation and condition were, by their nature, unpredictable. Furthermore, no two people are the same and, of course, there is no right way to travel life's path. There is no wrong way either. In *Speaking Our Minds*, Lisa Snyder writes, "A personal definition of Alzheimer's is as varied as the disease itself—as unique as the particular course it runs in each person who has it." While Dad was never diagnosed with Alzheimer's while he was alive, Snyder's description resonated with my sense that we would not find any clear answers by looking out into the world. We needed to find our way on our own.

I took solace in knowing that, while Dad's path was solely his, he did not need to travel it alone. That is, in fact, the only thing I had to go on as I became his primary caregiver. I could ensure appropriate autonomy and care and provide companionship and joy while he followed an otherwise very lonely and isolating trail. When I fell into step with my dad's journey with dementia, I did not have any idea where we were going, how we would get there, or what we would encounter. But we would travel together with attention to the moments that would arise along the way.

Even now as I recall the steps of our journey from beginning to end, I cannot chart this wilderness for anyone else. I can only cast a flashlight beam down the dark path, shining light on pieces of our story as comfort and company for other families navigating the twists and turns of their own caregiving landscape.

❧ 1 ❧

Without a Map

Adapting to a Changing Life

Throughout my twenties and thirties, as I embraced the responsibilities of adulthood, I navigated the literal wildernesses of the earth, deeply immersed in the biology of North America and my own body. I hiked, kayaked, and canoed through the northern United States and Alaska. I met my future husband, Thomas, on the trail. We built and repaired trails high in the mountains and deep in forests. Working with teens and young adults, we matched the rhythms of our lives to the flow and demands of the landscape. Living in community and working hard both strengthened and broadened our bodies, minds, and hearts. The roots of our lives grew long and strong, stretching deep into the earth and reaching out to one another. From these interconnected roots, Thomas and I would grow into our future together.

During our early years in Alaska, we became careful wilderness travelers. We relished the detailed planning of a route, studying maps for days before a trip. We organized menus to ensure that we had plenty of food but not too much weight to carry. Most importantly, after all of our careful preparations, when we stepped onto the trail at the beginning of a trip, we set aside all expectations and intentions. We were ready to meet whatever blessings or challenges arose along the way.

A few years after we met, Thomas and I spent a summer working on a trail maintenance crew for a remote Forest Service ranger district. Each week we traveled to and from our work sites by boat or floatplane. Traveling by plane was an exercise in precision, patience, and acceptance. We had to pack precisely to be within the plane's weight limits while also having the tools, fuel, and food we needed for the trip. We transported only the tools we anticipated needing for a project and no more, but we always packed an extra day's worth of food in case weather kept the plane from picking us up on schedule. After all of our careful attention to detail, we remained at the mercy of many elements beyond our control. We spent quite a few Monday mornings scrambling to get ready for our departure only to sit at the airport for hours waiting for the fog to lift enough for takeoff.

One week our crew was scheduled to do trail maintenance at a lake nestled high in the mountains. Our flight in was smooth, tucked between the morning's late-clearing fog and the afternoon's early storms. We unloaded quickly so the pilot could take off again before the clouds closed in on the narrow lake basin. As he flew off, we turned from the beach to haul our things up to the cabin that would be our base for the week and slowly absorbed our situation. The dense forest was cool and dark, there were bear tracks and scat everywhere, and the deep grooves and long, coarse hair in the cabin siding made it clear that our shelter had been used recently as a scratching post. We had been cohabitating with brown bears all summer, but something about this place felt different—not necessarily unsafe but definitely unpredictable. A feeling of unease settled into our bones that afternoon and remained with us all week. The dense understory of the forest, finicky mountain weather, and isolation of this camp were constant reminders that there were more elements outside of our sight and control than within it.

At the end of the week, we packed up early and brought our gear out to the beach to wait for the plane to pick us up. Sitting on the beach, away from the thick forest, the expanse of the sky gave us a wider and longer perspective. We were not only ready for a weekend of rest after the week's manual labor, we were eager for mental and emotional rest after living in the shadow that darkened this place. As the time of our pickup neared, we watched the sky and worried about the incoming weather. When the pilot made radio contact, he told us that he could see our valley as well as a bank of incoming clouds. It was going to be a close call, and he wanted us ready for a quick load-out. When we heard the plane engines, we stood and filled our arms, ready to pack the plane efficiently. The plane nudged over the ridge—and then turned away. The pilot radioed, "Not today. I hope you have an extra can of beans." We did, as always. That evening, as we cooked and ate our "emergency" meal, we embraced the unpredictability of our situation with new levity. Now that the shadowy "unknown" had manifested as a delay, the fear that we had been living with all week dissipated. In full acceptance of our vulnerability, the grip of anticipation and worry loosened. We remained ready to respond to the unexpected and had regained an ability to live fully within each moment.

In the wilderness, we embrace the challenge, beauty, and novelty of traveling through landscapes that are so much greater than ourselves. Navigation requires keen attention to the many external and internal conditions that will impact our trip. Our senses become attuned to weather, terrain, light, and dark and to our own abilities, preparation, courage, and will. With our attention so focused on our surroundings, we sink deeply into our bodies. Our bodies and minds become acutely responsive to both internal and external changes. We are instantly cooled and relieved from the heat and glare of the sun when we step into the shade. Our thighs burn from the degree of incline. We are as likely to be rendered breathless by our exertion as we are by the sweeping views that await us when we reach the peak of our ascent or discover a delicate wildflower at our feet.

My travels in the wilderness were rarely about the destination. Instead, each trip offered new ways of seeing and learning about the world and my place in it. While the expanse of a mountain range was a humbling and welcome reminder of how small I am within the vastness of the universe, I was empowered by the awareness of my finitude and emboldened to make each step meaningful. The accumulation of each new stride created powerful journeys that strengthened my sense of self and my commitment to living an authentic and meaningful life. Thomas and I have carried the lessons we learned from the wilderness into our parenting, our workplaces, and our communities in small towns and big cities.

In my forties, I leaned into these teachings while traveling through the wilderness of mind and heart. At the same time that my children entered their teenage years and Thomas's career grew wings, I became the primary family caregiver for my father. There wasn't a map for me to follow and I had not made any preparations for this trip. I often felt like I could not possibly have the skill, knowledge, or strength to competently meet the challenges that would inevitably arise. But, like all the other paths I had followed, it unfolded one step at a time. As it did, I not only supported my father's life journey, I enriched and grounded my own.

Into the Wilderness

As his confusion made it harder and harder for him to navigate, Dad built up a storehouse of anxiety, fear, and insecurity. He managed to get by through narrowing the walls of his world. After forty years of practicing law with the firm he had joined right after law school, he finally retired, but instead of flourishing in the time and space that opened up, he drew the curtains and brought his world even closer. In retrospect, his coping was quite masterful. He lived alone and managed his shifting abilities fairly well for several years.

My three brothers, Willy, Matthew, and Peter, and I had attributed his increasing reluctance to travel as simply a string of individual choices. We assumed he was playing less golf because his shoulder had gotten stiffer as arthritis settled into an old injury. We imagined he was losing weight because he walked daily and ate a very limited diet. In fact, all of these "choices" were really adaptations to his changing abilities. He could not have managed the logistics of arranging travel, much less have actually completed it. He could not track the passage of time, so he could not make and keep a lunch date or a tee time. Eventually, he stopped making or returning phone calls, likely because the conversations were too hard to follow. He lived for several years on a small bowl of cereal for breakfast and red peppers, carrots, and rotisserie chicken or frozen pizza for dinner, but it's likely that he simply began to forget to eat his meals.

As my brothers and I observed these lifestyle changes and their impacts on his life and comfort, we began to offer more and more support. In the beginning, we reached out on our own terms. When Dad stopped responding to emails, we returned to calling with updates. We mailed cards that, months later, I discovered he was reading over and over again. While they may have provided some company, our phone calls and mail never had context, so they probably just added to the confusion of his day. We wanted to believe that Dad was living his own life too. In fact, at some point, he had stopped living and had begun surviving.

The details of daily life had become tedious. Eating, dressing, shopping, and walking were his only activities, and they were all-consuming. The rituals and habits that at one point had brought a measure of security became obsessions. Without the ability to assimilate new information or stimuli, the only way he could remain comfortable was to repeat previously adopted behaviors. He was plagued by self-doubt and reconsidered everything he did multiple times. It could take forty-five minutes to wash his cereal bowl in the morning. Perhaps he could no longer track the beginning, middle, and end of this familiar process, or maybe he no longer trusted himself to do each step. Whatever the reason, every aspect of daily living required his painstaking attention. He was determined to be as independent as he was thorough, and he diligently and persistently attended to life's little details.

His world had shifted. It was hard to pinpoint the source or the causes, but it was clear to me and my brothers that everything was becoming a challenge. He seemed vaguely aware of it and only periodically annoyed by it. We patiently told him where to put away the dishes in his own kitchen when we visited and silently wondered how they got put away when we were not there. Dad lightheartedly told stories of putting clothes on in the wrong order, laughing as he recalled how awkward it felt when he pulled his long underwear on over his khaki pants. He described going back to the grocery store four times in one day to buy soap. Each time he got to the store, he was not sure if he really needed it so would go home to check. When I asked whether he had eventually decided to buy it or not, he didn't know. The slippers that were at his feet were either invisible or unrecognizable until I said, "Here they are," and pushed them closer to his toes. He seemed aware that he had once been able to make meaning of a digital clock and knew that the device told the time, but he could no longer translate the LED lights. He would point at the clock and ask, "What time is it?" When I answered, he would nod at my response, gracefully accepting that I had access to information that was no longer available to him.

My brothers and I worried about him, wondering how we could help and if we even should. He was a grown man. It wasn't our place to tell our own father how he should live his life, but surely this was not how he had envisioned enjoying retirement. In his narrow and protected world, there was no room for activities or relationships. One of us visited monthly so he had some periodic company, but he was alone most of the time. I began to help with medical appointments and paying bills. The four of us talked often about when we were supposed to intervene. We settled on watchful waiting, hoping it would be clear if and when we should step in.

I began to spend more and more time with Dad, but he lived in Connecticut and I was in Maine. It was a five-hour drive each way. In order to provide meaningful personal support as well as help with finances and medical appointments, I needed to be there for an extended period of time, and I wanted to make the most of each long drive. I began spending one five-day weekend per month with Dad. He was happy to have my company but, more than that, incredibly grateful for the way I supported life's daily work. It took a long time for him to get dressed in the morning or make his own breakfast, but he got through all of the steps eventually. I stayed out of the way so he could complete as many tasks as possible on his own. I learned to be patient and recognized that there was much greater value in his process than in the eventual outcome. The tasks that used to fit into small pockets of time in a busy life were now the cornerstones of his day. While I was careful to make time and space for Dad's independence and perseverance, he praised my efficiency and organization as we took care of business each day: Get the newspaper. Eat breakfast. Get an oil change for the car. Pay bills. Call to confirm the next eye doctor appointment. Eat lunch. Take a long walk. Go grocery shopping. Eat dinner. Wash the dishes.

At the time, we were just doing what needed to be done. But below the surface of these tasks, we were building a foundation of mutual trust, safety, and understanding that would hold us in good stead for the next few years. Dad did not often ask for help, but he would accept any contributions I made gratefully and gracefully. As I learned to identify what had gone missing in his life and mind, I was better able to anticipate and subtly meet his unfulfilled needs.

One of those missing pieces was the laundry. He never had any dirty laundry, but I also never saw him using the washing machine. One weekend, I finally realized he was handwashing his underpants and undershirts in the sink nightly and no longer washing his outer garments at all. He hung the outer garments over a railing to air out each night. I tried to explain that it would probably be a good idea to wash them in the machine, but he would not be convinced. He was sure that by airing them out nightly, he was doing what he had always done. I began to take away his dirty clothes while he was in the shower and leave a pile of clean clothes in their place. He always put them on without comment. Each time I visited, I went through drawers and closets and washed whatever looked or smelled like it needed to be cleaned. The soap was probably never fully rinsed out of his hand-washed undergarments, and airing out his pants, shirts, and sweaters would probably have been fine for a day or two, but not for weeks. By itself, this just sounds like bad hygiene, but he also had angry rashes all over his arms, back, and abdomen. Occasionally the rash crept up the back of his neck and peeked out of his shirt collar. He was uncomfortable and had sought help from his general practitioner, Dr. Berndt, but neither he nor the dermatologist to whom he referred Dad could figure out what was causing the rashes or how to resolve them. Finally, I was spending enough time with him to stumble upon the laundry situation. More frequent and thorough laundering didn't calm the rashes right away, but it did make them much less severe.

Dad had visits every few months with a urologist who checked bladder and kidney health and an eye doctor who monitored the slow progression of his glaucoma.

While the appointments were routine from the doctors' perspectives, they were stressful for Dad. Both doctors were kind, patient, and thorough, but with their busy schedules, there was not enough time to operate at a pace slow enough for Dad to navigate. I could see Dad's facial expressions change as he lost track of their explanations or instructions. We learned by trial and error where the line was between autonomy and dependence at these appointments. At one time, Dad had easily followed the instructions for leaving a urine sample; then one day he wandered the hallways for ten minutes with his empty cup, unsure of where he was or what he was supposed to be doing. I began to escort him to the bathroom and wait outside while he completed the task. Eventually I went into the bathroom to guide him through each step. With my words, actions, and eye contact, I attempted to support him in a way that allowed him to maintain some degree of privacy and control. I was painfully aware of these boundaries and did not want to overstep them, even as they shifted. Dad was just glad to be able to fulfill the doctor's request, likely hoping that his compliance would resolve the issues that kept us coming back.

One of his appointments was for a routine colonoscopy. The night before, at Dad's request, I ate a big dinner to "keep my energy up." We played Scrabble to pass the time in between his trips to the bathroom. I had been hopeful that with the night's colonoscopy prep in addition to the confusion that made it hard for him to track time and language in daily life, I would have a chance to finally beat him at the word game we had played together for decades. To my surprise, he won handily as usual, and we both celebrated his victory with a cheer. We held on to the festive spirit of the game through the evening and into the next morning as we got ready for the appointment. Once at the office, however, Dad became more and more subdued. Changed into a hospital gown and ready for the procedure, Dad moved to a small curtained room, and I accompanied him. Our conversation turned serious. Perhaps it was the vulnerability of sitting in a hospital gown, the result of not eating for twenty-four hours, or the fear and anticipation of anesthesia, but he needed to talk about family, health, life, and death. He acknowledged a few relationships that had grown sour and hard to maintain and that he wished to heal. He expressed regret over his own father's frailty and death and his deep sadness over his mom's more recent death, though he appreciated the gentleness of her passing. He wanted to be sure I understood he wanted to live out his life as naturally as possible and did not want medical interference to prolong it. His intensity and gravity required me to enter and respond from that same space of presurgery vulnerability. I realized how much trust he had in me and how much emotional weight he was sharing with me; I repeated back everything I had heard and promised him I would uphold his wishes. I reminded him we had been to his former law office the day before to complete a medical power of attorney so that I would be able to do that legally when the time came. As we sat there together that morning, I absorbed anew the heft of responsibility I was accepting by stepping in as Dad's companion and caregiver. Later that afternoon, when the fog of anesthesia faded, he apologized for having been so serious and weighty. He worried that, in his nervousness, he had been inappropriate or even silly in his sharing. I assured him that I welcomed his openness and honesty and I appreciated our conversation. I had gained new appreciation for our deepening relationship.

My visits with Dad grew longer and more frequent. It had become clear that my time with him met critical needs for safety and health as well as comfort and happiness. Thomas and our two sons, Duncan and Thatcher, held down the fort at home, and I was grateful to have an understanding employer who did not mind how often I was absent as long as my work got done. But the balance in my life was shifting. I often felt like I was giving everyone a little, but nobody was getting all they truly needed from me. While everyone else was incredibly supportive, I harbored a nagging reluctance to fully honor the skillful, challenging, and necessary work I was doing on behalf of Dad. I knew the resistance that I felt did not accurately reflect the actual time or energy I spent with Dad. It took me a few months to identify it, but I finally found the source of my hesitation: This was not *a job*. I was not earning income for it and had no real job description. Yet I could see and feel clearly that it was hard work. And my family could see and feel it too. It was apparent to them during my long weekends away from home. It was obvious to them in the tears, worry, and exhaustion I carried back from each visit. As a family, we had to confront the cultural norm that devalues family caregiving and declare its importance and prominence in our lives.

When I became a parent, I was shocked to realize how little attention and support our communities offer for the critical social function of raising children. In the early months, I felt indignant about the heft of my new responsibilities and the world's obliviousness. As time went on, my rage melted away, and I bore the responsibilities of family and work quietly along with everyone else. But here it was again at the other end of the spectrum of life. Our elders deserve the same levels of attention and engagement as anyone else, young or old or in between. Many older adults require as much physical and emotional care as toddlers and newborns. Once I began caring for my dad, I found out how few resources are available—and again how little attention is paid—to the family members carrying the responsibility of caring up the generational ladder.

Once I claimed the value and authority of the work I felt called to do for Dad, I applied myself to caregiving wholeheartedly. Slowly, I began to let go of what was less important. I whittled my hours down at work from full-time to half-time and finally quarter-time. I talked with Thomas and the boys about the pull I felt to provide better support for Dad. With their reassurances and blessing, I began to release some of the guilt I felt when I was not with them and embrace the time I spent with Dad as necessary and meaningful.

Still, it quickly became evident that even these longer, more frequent weekend visits were not enough. Not only was Dad not taking care of himself, he could not or would not relearn self-care habits that had faded. When my brothers or I tried to approach him about his waning capabilities, he assured us that he was fine. We talked with him more often about downsizing, moving closer to one of us, or exploring assisted living. We affirmed his self-concept that he was "fine" but introduced the idea that there could come a time when he might need or want some support. We advocated for moving sooner rather than later so that he would be settled somewhere new before that time came. Whenever I brought up a move, he told me he just needed my little bit of help every once in a while. He offered to hire me as his personal assistant. I responded as though he had been joking, but he really wasn't. He was always so relieved when I took care of things, and no matter how full he felt our agenda was, we always managed plenty of time for walks, talks, and lighthearted laughter. It would have been a great job had we not lived five hours apart.

Then the day arrived when it was crystal clear that it was time to step in. My periodic help and watchful waiting were no longer safe.

Going in Circles

My youngest brother, Peter, was living in Massachusetts, equidistant between Dad and me. He was a music professor, and Dad had always enjoyed his concerts. When the time came for his first performance with a new ensemble, Peter sent Dad directions to the theater and we all made plans to meet a few hours before the concert. We would have dinner and a chance to visit before the show. Dad would spend the night at Peter's house in the next town and drive home the next day in the light. He had been to Peter's house dozens of times so most of the route was familiar. The only deviation from habit was meeting at the concert hall a few miles away.

Our rendezvous time came and went. Dad did not answer his cell phone. That did not surprise us; he didn't always recall how to use his cell phone, and he would never try to answer it while driving. Over the course of two hours, we must have called eight to ten times, leaving voicemail messages we knew he would never retrieve. He was not answering his home phone either, so we assumed he had left and was on his way but we had no idea where he was. Ten minutes before the curtain went up, he called Peter to say he was lost. Peter rushed out to the lobby where the rest of us were still waiting nervously. It took some detective work to figure out where Dad was. The only thing he could tell us was that he was in a gas station parking lot, and he tried repeatedly to explain how he had gotten there. He had clearly not been following my brother's directions for some time. Finally, we asked him to look out the window and tell us exactly what he saw. Fortunately, he could read a street sign and the gas station sign, and we plugged them into a GPS. We identified the location—approximately twenty minutes away—and told him to stay where he was until we got there. Thomas left to retrieve him, Peter got onstage, and the rest of us sat down to watch the concert.

I was not convinced that Dad would remember the phone conversation and stay where he was, but thankfully, he did. Dad was very happy to see Thomas pull up next to him and offer to lead him to the concert hall in a slow caravan. They arrived before intermission. He was a little shaken about being lost but more curious about how he had misinterpreted the directions. The rest of us were alarmed by the fact that he had been lost for several hours before it occurred to him to stop and call for help. Since he seemed unscathed, we tried not to share our alarm, but we had learned some valuable lessons about Dad's limitations. He could not navigate to unfamiliar places alone any longer. Since we were the only ones he would be visiting, we now had a responsibility to actually keep him from traveling outside of his comfort zone.

The rest of the weekend was without incident, including his return home the next day. In a stroke of preventative brilliance, Peter connected Dad's phone to the Find My iPhone app and shared the login information with all of us. If we ever had concerns about his safety or whereabouts in the future, it would be easier to find him.

This backup plan relied on Dad keeping his phone with him, but it was a start.

Feeling as though we had reached a dead end in trying to talk Dad into moving and not wanting to alienate him, we sought support from Dr. Berndt. Dad had a healthy respect for authority, and we hoped that if his doctor voiced concern about his cognitive changes, he might be more open to establishing some practical support at home or changing his living situation. Both Peter and I had several conversations with Dr. Berndt on the phone expressing our concern and asking him to do a cognitive evaluation. We told him about the concert episode and our worry that Dad was still driving and still living alone. I described my weekend visits and observations. We explained that Dad would be more willing to hear about these issues and possible solutions from Dr. Berndt because of his medical expertise. Dad's next visit with him was only a few weeks after the concert. After a review of vital signs, blood and urine tests, and an examination of the rashes, the doctor asked Dad how he felt he was managing his daily affairs, inquiring specifically about cooking, paying the bills, and driving. Dad said, "Fine. I'm fine." As Dr. Berndt stood up, I realized that was the end of the conversation. My eyes went wide and I slowly shook my head at Dr. Berndt. I willed him to hear me yelling my thoughts at him, *Things are not fine. Ask a better question! Pay attention!* He told my dad to call him if he had any concerns and ushered us out the door with a weak smile.

I found out later that Dad had missed multiple follow-up visits with Dr. Berndt in the previous year. He had shown up at his office when he was supposed to be at urology. The day before a scheduled appointment, he would go into the office multiple times to confirm his appointment. He had been a patient in that office for over five years and had never behaved that way before. These new and unusual behaviors should have been red flags that merited attention and action for every receptionist, medical assistant, and doctor in the building. Despite that *and* our pleas for help, they either didn't notice or wouldn't acknowledge that he was changing. The office never raised the possibility of dementia, and Dr. Berndt never offered Dad a cognitive evaluation. They never assessed him for anxiety or depression. Dr. Berndt's help was limited to referrals to urologists and dermatologists for recurring UTIs and rashes. These extra appointments and unfamiliar people just added layers of stress and confusion to Dad's life while addressing only symptoms rather than identifying the underlying problems. What Dad really needed was daily oversight, support for personal hygiene, and a plan for the inevitable changes to come. I was frustrated with the medical team around us but wary of trying to start over. Meanwhile, I was spending more and more time visiting Dad, shuttling him to appointments, and trying to strategize new ways to keep him safe and comfortable. We were on our own in unfamiliar territory.

I was now on the phone with my brothers almost weekly. We knew the concert incident was a warning signal. Our periodic visits would no longer be enough, and it was time to step in. We wanted to convince Dad to move closer. If he were a few hours nearer to me, Peter, and Matthew, we could each check in on him more often. Ideally, he could live somewhere in between the three of us, and we could give him more frequent company and a little more help. Dad would benefit from the support of a community. With extra eyes to watch and offer guidance when needed, he would preserve as much independence as he could for as long as possible. We hatched a plan we hoped would win him over.

I began visiting residential care facilities. As I toured various independent living, assisted living, and memory care residences, I tried to discern where Dad's needs would fall within this continuum of care. Dad did not need medical care; he just needed extra eyes and a modest amount of support. But I also knew that what I saw as support, he would look on as intrusion. Having always been a private person, Dad would want to maintain his personal space. It seemed feasible he could move into an independent living facility and still feel comfortable, and I looked for a place that would feel like home. I visited places where the staff were friendly, but the hallways were empty. They felt like hotels. It didn't seem very helpful to live in a communal environment if staff and residents maintained habits of isolation. These places were easy to cross off of my list. In other facilities, I was drawn to positive energy from residents and staff and active social programs, but I wondered if they would offer enough privacy to suit Dad. It was going to be a delicate balance.

Meanwhile, we also began to look for bids to repair leaky pipes and a damaged ceiling at Dad's condominium. We proposed a short-term move into an independent living apartment while the condo repairs were being done. We reasoned that the project would only get bigger the longer he waited, so it would be optimal to get it completed over that winter. We sold the virtues of relocating to a place away from the work zone where all of his needs would be met and he wouldn't have to worry as much about the travel hazards and shoveling of a New England winter. Most compelling, we promised to find a place closer to three of his four children so that he would get to see all of us, and his grandchildren, more often.

He was not excited about the prospect of change but he was willing to play along. We arranged visits to two graduated care facilities during a weekend when my brothers and I could go with him. It was the beginning of a holiday weekend, and we hoped to intersperse enough family time and festivities among the visits to offer a distraction from the inevitable stress they would stimulate. As we toured each place and during the drives in between them, we had opportunities to discuss the benefits of a move as well as to hear and appreciate Dad's hesitation and reluctance. We saw independent living cottages and apartments as well as assisted living units. He liked the autonomy of the cottages but knew he didn't need or want that much space. We talked about services and care available at each facility as well as options for contracting with outside agencies. He clearly felt more comfortable in the independent living environments, but he was also warming to the idea that he might need support in the future. He was pleasant and courteous with the staff members we met at each facility, though a bit uncomfortable with being the center of attention.

In the independent living building at Rosen Springs, he seemed genuinely at ease. At Rosen Springs, care services could be brought to an individual independent living apartment or, depending on needs, a resident could move to the assisted living or memory care neighborhoods onsite. The facility contained a circle of cottages, an independent living building, and the assisted living/memory care building connected by sidewalks and open space. The whole complex felt open, walkable, and inviting. In its open containment, it felt comforting and expansive rather than confining, even to Dad. The apartments were clean and full of natural light. Residents and staff were friendly, and the halls hummed with gentle, positive energy. My brothers and I were enthusiastic. Dad said, "I'll think about it." We spent the evening together at Matthew's house and enjoyed conversation, good food, and the antics of all seven grandchildren playing together. We were ready to relax. My brothers and I figured we would strategize about how to get Dad to Rosen Springs later.

The next day, "later" became an urgent "now." Just six weeks after getting lost on the way to the concert, Dad got mixed up on his way home. He left Matthew's house following Peter. He planned to peel away at a familiar highway junction and proceed home from there. He was confident he would recognize it and be able to make his way back to his condominium while Peter continued on to his house. Unfortunately, they became disconnected early, and Dad never made it to that familiar junction on the highway. When Peter called to let us know that he had lost sight of him in the rearview mirror, we quickly connected to Dad's Find My iPhone account. We watched our phones in horror as the little blue dot on the map representing Dad retraced a section of highway over and over again. I imagine he was looking for something familiar and was unaware he was repeating the same forty-five miles of highway in a triangular pattern. We worried that he had probably not stopped for food, water, or gas. Nightfall and a snowstorm were approaching, and we were concerned he could become a danger to himself and to others while navigating roads that were dark, snowy, and unfamiliar.

We thought about calling the police and then realized that wouldn't help. None of us knew his license plate number. We decided to try to intercept him. Peter drove up from Massachusetts, and Willy and Matthew drove down from New Hampshire. As they approached his vehicle from opposite sides of the divided highway, we began to wonder how they were going to get him to pull over. Then, as if responding to our silent pleas, the blue dot on our maps stopped. Dad had pulled into a Dunkin' Donuts. When Peter walked in a few minutes later, Dad was pleasantly surprised to see him and offered to buy him a sandwich. It did not seem odd to him that they should run into each other there after losing track of one another forty miles away and several hours earlier. When Willy and Matthew arrived a few minutes later, Dad was grateful for Willy's offer to drive him the rest of the way home. It was dark and beginning to snow. He did not seem aware that he had been lost nor that he had been found. Willy and Matthew took Dad the remaining three hours home, got him settled in, and then drove the five hours back north to New Hampshire. It was a close call that left us all very uneasy. We needed to act more quickly.

The next day, I called Rosen Springs. When I visited Dad a few days later, I told him I had put him on the waiting list for an independent living apartment. He was annoyed and unconvinced the temporary winter move was necessary, despite my assurance that it was the right thing to do. He wanted to know why he needed to relocate and why I was so sure it needed to be now. I told him that he had gotten lost on the drive back from New Hampshire. I described how scary it was to follow his path on the map, watching him driving in circles. His eyes got wide and he agreed that it sounded scary, but his unease came from not recollecting the incident at all: he believed me, but he had absolutely no memory of it. Then he tried to convince me that getting lost had been an outlier, that he could avoid it in the future by not going anywhere. He assured me that he would just stay close to home and everything would be OK. As he said this, we were driving in his neighborhood. He was behind the wheel and I was the navigator, which had been our usual arrangement for months. It allowed me to simultaneously assess how well he could attend to the mechanics of driving and how much navigational support he needed. We were stopped at a red light at a railroad crossing. He looked around and said, "But I know this area so well." And for a moment, I hesitated. He was still driving very well and never needed my help with directions when we were in the vicinity of his condo, the grocery store, the post office, and other familiar haunts. He did seem fine—for today. Finally, I told him I didn't know what it meant that he had gotten lost, but that it worried me. "I'm worried that the day might come when it all seems unfamiliar," I said. "It scares me that you could be alone and not know how to get home or how to get help to get home."

He looked surprised for a brief moment. Then, sadly, he agreed. "That would scare me too," he said quietly. We had gotten somewhere. He knew something was changing for him. Maybe he was already scared. This moment of awareness and acceptance was the opening we needed to make a change. I explained that moving to Rosen Springs for the winter would be a first step, a trial while the condo was being repaired. At Rosen Springs, he would be in southern Maine, only one and a half hours away from Matthew, Peter, and me. We could each visit him more often. I would take care of all of the moving details and make sure he felt safe, comfortable, and settled in there.

He reluctantly agreed, and I breathed a sigh of relief. His consent was so important.

We would repeat this conversation several times as we made preparations, but the reluctance that showed up from time to time seemed to be more out of frustration and dislike for his situation than out of dislike for the response to it. It took six weeks to get off the waiting list and there were a lot of tense moments in those weeks. Dad seemed to grasp that change was afoot, but did not retain when, why, where, or how. When we did talk about a move, he was anxious about the steps to accomplish it. I reassured him often that I would take care of all of the details and be with him every step of the way. I coordinated as much of the logistics as possible out of sight and hearing range so that he simply wouldn't worry about it. We talked about anything other than moving and the unknowns that would accompany a change of scenery.

When the day finally came, the move was carefully orchestrated and went as smoothly as could be expected. I kept Dad engaged and calm with small sorting and packing tasks, while Matthew, Thomas, Duncan, and Thatcher quickly and quietly loaded the truck with the furniture we had decided to bring to simulate the appearance, function, and comfort of his living room and bedroom. We took the familiar corner cupboard, bookshelf, table, and rocking chair that had always been in his living room. The condo would still be furnished enough that it would be habitable if we were to return, but we were taking the pieces to Maine that would help his new apartment look and feel like home. The boys and the moving truck left quickly. Dad and I lingered to tie up a few loose ends and absorb the situation before following a little more slowly.

By the time we got to Rosen Springs four hours later, his living room and bedroom had been recreated, everything was unpacked, and the empty boxes were out of sight. Children, in-laws, and grandchildren were sitting in his living room watching golf while they waited for him. The apartment was full of his belongings and, more importantly, brimming with the people who loved him. It looked and sounded familiar from the moment we walked in. He knew that it was not home, but it was close.

Reorienting

Years earlier we had talked with Dad about moving closer when he retired. He even briefly entertained our offer to move in with us or to build a cottage on our land. He had the same conversation with Matthew. In the end, he always deflected. His desire for autonomy, and his wish for his children to have their independence, encouraged a boundary that kept us from making any move toward cohabitating. By the time it was clear Dad needed a new living situation, none of us were prepared to shift our lives as dramatically as would be required to bring Dad into our homes. Even if it had felt right for him or for one of us, we would not have been able to do it quickly enough. We were grateful to find a residence that would support Dad within the abilities he still had while preparing for and anticipating the new needs that would inevitably arise.

I stayed with Dad for the first week in his new apartment in independent living at Rosen Springs. As I helped him through this very challenging transition, I gained greater insight into the depth of the obstacles he had learned to live with. He had been living alone for over a decade, and navigating his condominium, neighborhood, and the rhythms of his day had become completely dependent on deeply ingrained habits. By the time he moved, he no longer tracked the passage of time on a calendar, but he went out to get a newspaper each morning and referred to the front page many times each day to identify the year, month, and day of the week. Mail delivery indicated it was time to eat lunch and finishing lunch meant it was time for a walk. He checked the stovetop to be sure all of the burners were off every time he walked through the kitchen. He had dozens of these deliberate and clever devices to order his days and protect autonomy, safety, and comfort. It had taken a lot of creativity to cultivate these coping mechanisms as they were needed. Learning to deal with the new environment at Rosen Springs meant establishing new routines and identifying new signposts to ensure he could make his way through the day.

In that first week, we attempted to embed familiarity, habit, and spatial awareness in his body rather than his mind. We walked the community hallways endlessly. He never knew where he was, when the hallway would end, or how long we had been walking. The paintings on the wall, community rooms, mailboxes, and offices marked the route along the corridor for me; they were always surprises to him. He never anticipated what was around the next corner. Nothing was familiar, nor would it become familiar with repeated encounters. He simply did not have the capacity to create new meaning or memory. But he was content to walk the halls with me in calm and trusting spirit. The few times he got angry or frustrated, he became critical and dismissive of me and anything within sight. I promised I would stay with him until it was all more comfortable and reminded him that we could enjoy being there and being together if we kept a positive outlook. He was always reassured and willing to try to recalibrate with a hug and a smile. Over that week, he did learn to trust that it was safe to go out the door and start walking. Once he took that first step, he would always find a caring resident or staff member. A few years later, when instinct and habit ceased to offer any help, he relied completely on the kindness of others in that same trusting and gentle spirit.

Once Dad was settled in at Rosen Springs, my worry subsided somewhat. Residing within a community simply seemed safer than living in isolation. There were eyes to observe and hands to help guide him toward safe, fulfilling, and, eventually, happily engaged days. But dementia had become a constant companion, and the only given was that Dad's capacity and connections would continue to change. Our concerns would change with them.

I was grateful to stop intervening and to step back and offer my support in a different way. It was humbling and often overwhelming to be responsible for another person's life and liberty. When I had been a new parent, I let trust and confidence in my sons guide my instincts. From breastfeeding to movement to words, I sensed that they knew what to do and I would know how to support them. Their instincts would keep them safe, healthy, and developing appropriately. I intervened enough to keep them from walking into traffic, tumbling down stairs, and choking on toys, but I also understood the significance of their developing independence. When one of my boys reached for a farther rung on the monkey bars, I would step a little closer, but not so close that my presence would cause him to doubt his abilities. I was on hand to provide guidance for safety, exploration, and joy, but took care not to squelch their developing courage and confidence.

In this same way, I became a guardian for Dad's experiences. I paid close attention to his actions and inactions in order to anticipate his needs and set us both up for positive interactions. Our relationship shifted in response to the change in landscape.

In the months after Dad moved to independent living, I became very aware of how meaningful each moment was for us both. Because Dad lacked the ability to create or store memories, each moment was fleeting. At times, this felt risky. We were always dangling our feet at the edge of an abyss and a misstep could create a moment that reinforced latent fear, sadness, or anxiety. Of course, each moment also had the potential to cultivate positive feelings of self-worth, joy, belonging, and security. I watched his actions and reactions carefully, striving to make our engagements positive, while also acknowledging the reality of his situation. He was occasionally aware of how dependent he had become on me to manage his personal affairs. He was often aware that he was in a living environment established for people who needed support but could not identify himself within that population. At the young age of sixty-eight, Dad was one of the few people in the building who navigated without the assistance of a cane, wheelchair, or walker. When the snow and ice melted, he was eager to resume daily walks. For the last few years, walking had become essential to his happiness, and he relied on the infusion of energy it generated. He explained that it helped to "clear the cobwebs" of his mind, which were getting thick. Without visible physical manifestations of the burdens he bore, many people could not see the challenges he faced, but he was the resident most likely to walk out the front door and not be able to get back to his apartment.

~

One day two decades earlier, I had stepped out of our cabin without a purpose or destination, just needing to walk. Thomas and I had gotten into a circular conversation that found us exactly 180 degrees away from one another and unable to reconcile our difference of opinion. Rather than continuing to try to talk a way to resolution, I left to walk my way to it. Perhaps I was "clearing the cobwebs" too. At the time, it felt like blowing off steam.

It was mid-afternoon. During an Alaskan winter, the sun never gets too high and sets early. Leaving the cabin at dusk to wander alone in the woods was either an act of boldness or stupidity. But I needed to move, and I needed to be alone. I stomped along with my hands jammed in my pockets and my head down, replaying the words of the discussion gone awry in my head. As I trudged along through territory that was familiar and some that was not, my footsteps slowly got lighter and my head lifted. I noticed the bite of the cold air and the encroaching darkness just as I came to a cluster of trees Thomas and I had named the Grove of the Patriarchs.

The Grove of the Patriarchs was a stand of Sitka spruce that towered above the rest of that forest. We guessed that the roots of these magnificent trees reached down to a spring that kept them better hydrated than the vegetation of the surrounding area. This grove was so physically distinct from the rest of the forest it felt imbued with a mystical or spiritual power. When I walked into it that evening, I was enveloped in a warm hug. The grove was thick enough to block the wind so there may have been a true change of air temperature, but I also had a sudden shift in perception. I was no longer alone. I was protected by the patriarchs, embraced by their care, integrity, and quiet strength.

I looked down at the winding serpentine roots at my feet and up into the tops of the trees. The trees supported me and also towered over my five-foot frame. Keenly aware of my smallness, I grew still. I was humbled and grateful simply to be present. The conversation that had precipitated my angry walk had melted away. Whatever lingering trifles I carried in my mind were inconsequential when exposed to the vast sky and protective canopy. With each step I had taken into the woods, I moved closer to appreciation and acceptance of a world beyond my control and understanding. I was ready to return to the cabin, offer my apologies, and start anew. I knew the way home.

2

Along the Way

Peering through the Windows of Change

When Thomas and I bought a small piece of land in Alaska, we wanted a home base from which we could continue to explore the wilderness. Our version of developing the land was fairly minimalistic: we envisioned a parking spot, an outhouse, and a tepee connected by narrow footpaths. Thomas had lived in the tepee before, and it was among the few possessions he had piled into his truck and brought with him when he came north. It took us several weeks to fell eight birch trees and peel them into strong, straight poles to support the heavy canvas. We built a wide platform to provide a base for the floor. The platform would keep us warmer by elevating us off the ground and would protect the integrity of the fabric. Days got shorter and colder more quickly than we had anticipated that fall. Light rain drizzled from the sky almost daily, saturating our clothing and making tools slippery. I kept a handful of candy in my shirt pocket to give me extra fuel and good cheer throughout each long, hard day. We were warmed by our work and constant movement during the day, but it was cold and damp in our backpacking tent at night. We hoped to have the tepee up before the first snowfall of the season.

We raised the tepee and installed the woodstove on my birthday in late October. We celebrated with a hearty dinner and a glass of wine, anticipating a good night's sleep. That night the pitter-patter of rain gave way to the silence of snow softly falling. The tepee shed several inches of snow beautifully. Unfortunately, it also seemed to shed heat. Over the next few days, we realized that the space we had been so eager to stretch out into was impossible to warm in the damp coldness of Southeast Alaska. We continued to spend our days working outside, cutting and splitting firewood for the long heating season ahead. Our evenings were reduced to quick dinners before cuddling under piles of blankets and sleeping bags to try to stay warm for the night. Our sleep in the tepee was fitful. We could hear everything and see nothing. The white, windowless, round structure felt suffocating. When we heard heavy footsteps crunching in the snow at night, we imagined bears wandering by curiously. Unable to interpret the sounds, we became fearful, nervous, and uncertain about our ability to live in this wilderness. We shared the land with large brown bears, wily black bears, and gangly moose. We were sleeping right next to our camp kitchen. We would never have cooked and eaten so close to our bedding if we were backpacking, yet we did it in the oversize tent we had made into our home. If any of the local bears wanted our salmon leftovers before heading to the mountains for a sleepy winter, they could have barged right in. The moose that frequented our newly made trails didn't see well. We worried they would stumble into the side of the tepee, which would have been indistinguishable in the whiteout of the falling snow. We didn't want to wake up to 600 pounds of company of either variety.

We were fortunate to have one another and tried to talk each other into feeling more comfortable, but when a neighbor offered to help us build a small cabin, we eagerly accepted. Again, we worked hard, long days. During our short stint in the tepee, we had learned a lot about our comfort and safety needs. We designed and built a cabin with large windows that was off of the ground and easy to heat. We were grateful to move into our ten-by-twelve-foot home just a month later, several days before Thanksgiving. When we looked out our windows to the beauty of the land both day and night, we reclaimed trust in the land and confidence in our ability to navigate it. We continued to spend the majority of every day outdoors, but before we went out each morning and when we returned to the cabin each evening, we now had space for a different kind of work.

The cabin was not only a base for exploration, it was also a great place for contemplation and reflection. It provided a literal window onto the wilderness outside as well as a figurative window into our hearts, motivations, and inspirations. Each time we looked out to garner a sense of what was happening around us, we also gained a sense of ourselves and our place within the world. We kept daily journal entries that logged the weather, temperature, our moods, and a daily poem. Our intention to pay attention to the big picture—the world outside the window—inevitably drew us to also pay close attention to ourselves and each moment as it arose.

In my time with Dad, the windows of perspective resembled a kaleidoscope as his view to the world outside also mingled with the window to the world of the heart.

Past and future collided with the present. Each scene was a brief one, though no less beautiful or heartbreaking for its impermanence. Learning to experience Dad's sense of the world gave me my own bittersweet window of perspective, like the bright warmth of the sun through a frosty winter pane.

Looking Back

I had gotten glimpses of Dad's narrowing window to the world during the last few months he was still in his condominium. For years we had talked on the phone weekly. Whenever I had a visit coming up, I would let him know my arrival date a week in advance. After the first time my arrival took him by surprise, I began calling the night before as well. Eventually, I stopped giving him advance notice. It seemed that he would remember only that something was going to happen, but not what or when. This made him very anxious. To avoid causing confusion, I would call twice on my way down: once when I left my house and once when I was within an hour of his condo. On one of these visits, I got stuck in traffic and had to call several times from the road to give an updated ETA. When I finally arrived, exhausted from driving through the rain in Friday evening traffic, he was peering out the window through the curtains. "What took you so long?" he asked abruptly. "Traffic," I replied just as curtly. Then, noticing the tension in the air and anxiety on his face, I added more softly, "I brought dinner. Let's eat." I suspect that he had been waiting anxiously at the window since my first call and had no recollection of the half dozen more conversations we had had in the intervening six hours. Later this visit, we drove up to Maine together and signed the paperwork to secure his apartment rental at Rosen

Springs. He made it clear that he was not happy about it, but he was willing to give it a try. I took that acceptance, despite the reluctance, to mean that somewhere amid the confusion and the worry, this strong, independent, and reserved man knew we were on the right path.

A few weeks later, we worked on the resident profile paperwork for Rosen Springs together. We were at the condominium sitting in the dim light of the kitchen surrounded by piles of expired coupons, mail, and newspapers. Dad was vacillating between anxiety over the impending move and comfort at the methodical way we were moving through business details. He was no longer reading or writing with any fluidity, so I acted as secretary, reading the questions to him and recording his responses. By taking care of the mechanical aspects of the application with ease, I hoped that Dad's participation in the content might support his sense of self-determination and inspire some enthusiasm for the upcoming change. He answered the basics easily enough: name, address, date of birth. He provided his parents' names, as well as those of his two sisters and three sons. Then the form asked where else he had lived. He paused. I waited.

"I've always lived here, haven't I?" There was doubt in his voice, but he didn't have any concrete memories to suggest he had ever lived anywhere other than in his condominium in that town. I confirmed that he had lived in other places and encouraged him to think about when he was a boy, where he had gone to school. He suddenly recalled with relief that he had lived in France. I mentioned a few other places from his childhood and early adulthood: Washington State, Washington, DC, and Connecticut. "Oh yes," he nodded with a very slight glimmer of recognition.

Then I mentioned the house in Bridgewater. He shook his head and his forehead creased. "I don't know that one," he said. I told him he had lived there for twenty-five years. I had grown up there with my three brothers. He shook his head. He had no idea what I was talking about. "Tell me about it," he suggested. I took a deep breath and swallowed my surprise and tears. I told him again how long he had lived there. I described the color, size, features, and location of the house in the center of town. It was a large, old, gray Victorian, always in need of work but stately and full of life. He had raised four children there. We ran through the halls, roller-skated around the big wraparound porch, and played Ping-Pong in the attic. We puzzled over many games of Scrabble and Monopoly by the fireplace in the living room. The house had deep closets and other nooks and crannies for games of hide-and-seek on rainy days. The yard had big old trees for climbing and building forts. This house, my childhood home, held fairy-tale proportions in my mind. It didn't exist at all in his. He listened with interest and curiosity as though I were telling him a story, but he had no sense of it being *his* story. I offered to drive him past it on another weekend when we had more time. He was intrigued and said, "I'd like that."

We moved on and continued to address the questions in the application, but I had come across new insight into how fragile his awareness of himself and the world around him had become. For many months, I had been bristling at naming Dad's challenges "memory loss." Now I finally saw why. Along with losing his memory, he was losing his identity. If memory holds our experiences, history, values, challenges, successes, and relationships, it is the guardian of our sense of connection in the world. I suddenly worried for him in a new way. If his window to the world contained only the present moment without the accumulated learning and context of his past, how would he create meaning in the days, months, and years ahead?

As Dad's capacities changed, vivid memories from his childhood emerged. He shared the stories over and over again, snippets of experience that crystallized vividly for a short time in his mind, offering temporary benchmarks of history and links to the present. The memories were vivid and visceral while they lasted, but when they evaporated, they were gone without a trace. During one visit, he told me of his early teen years in boarding school, particularly reveling in the fun he and his classmates took in sliding down the smooth hardwood floor. It was a game they all enjoyed until he slid into the steam radiator at the other end and came away with an imprint of the heater in his forehead. The memory made him laugh out loud at their antics and then wince and tenderly touch his forehead as he remembered the pain. Another time, he shared a story from his early elementary school years in France. He had felt humiliated when he was reprimanded for drinking water during class but licked his lips recalling how thirsty he had been when he chose to break the rule. He seemed to revive and then release memories from his life one at a time, working backward. By the time I noticed the pattern, adulthood was long gone and the childhood memories that emerged were from ever younger ages.

This progression back through memories paralleled a regression in capabilities that had developed, it seemed to me, more or less around the same time. I may have been trying to impose order where none existed, but it was interesting to pay attention to his abilities in the context of whatever memories were alive in him at the time. When he recalled the story of the water bottle in France, he was counting and naming objects in French. I wondered if he was going to lose his ability to speak English and revert to French altogether. I watched as he read newspaper headlines or menus, struggling to sound out words. Would he forget how to read? I wondered if the unlearning that he seemed to be experiencing would mirror the way in which he had gained his knowledge and experience.

Speaking had become hard for Dad too. Whereas initially he periodically had trouble finding the right word to complete a sentence, now he was having trouble finding the right words to engage in a conversation or express himself at all. I could not tell if the challenge was in verbalizing his thoughts or in no longer having the words to name and organize thoughts in his mind. I considered the way that my sons had acquired language and cognitive skills. Expression and intention preceded language in the baby years. Soon, vocalizations became words, which grew into conversations. By two, they could interpret pictures, and by four they were reading simple words. Throughout these developments, their expanding perspective fostered an ability to understand and explore the world around them. I tried to imagine how the process would work in reverse and wondered how tightly Dad's current experiences of the world were interwoven with his ability to interpret and explain them verbally.

I began to share my observations, experiences, and questions in long, rambling emails to my brothers and Aunt Julie, Dad's younger sister. Even though I saw Dad most often and could offer personal observations about his changes, everyone was concerned and interested in being involved. We all wished that Dad could have enjoyed the retirement full of grandchildren, golf, and travel he had always envisioned. But he couldn't. Fortunately, the memory of that aspiration was long gone for him so he did not hold regret either. Once the rest of us put aside our own sadness for the future that he would never have, we focused our energy on establishing and maintaining an optimal situation for Dad within his remaining capacities. While each email brought them into the process and assured me that I wasn't alone, writing also gave me a chance to digest and absorb the experiences I shared with Dad. As I wrote, I gained a degree of perspective unclouded by my emotional responses. Sometimes the moments with Dad were sweet and tender, sometimes devastating. When I told them about something challenging, sharing helped me to own my experience of it while also liberating me from its weight. As I relived and reconsidered a joyful experience with Dad, I appreciated it for what it was: a single moment in time. There were no emergency exits available for us to duck out of the hard times, and there were no tethers for holding on to the good times. Though I still often felt helpless and in way over my head, retelling these episodes convinced me that simply staying present was enough. It was, in fact, all I could do.

While each correspondence gave me an opportunity to notice and acknowledge the hard work of caregiving and reaffirm my commitment to it, each email was also an invitation to my brothers and aunt to participate in the process. Julie wrote back long and thoughtful responses that encouraged different ways of looking at Dad's situation. She had supported my grandparents when Dad's dad had declined with Alzheimer's decades earlier. She asked questions about care, medication, and behavior management from a perspective honed through prior experience. My oldest brother, Willy, lived farthest away and could not visit as often as he would have liked. He always responded to my messages with encouragement and gratitude, aware of the responsibility I was carrying on behalf of all of us. As time went on, I craved the energetic sharing of the weight of Dad's situation more than the feedback. I envisioned that by distributing what I knew, I would also somehow parcel out the weight of that knowing. And if we could each hold more, perhaps Dad would have less to carry. I pictured my brothers and aunt responding to his changing capacities and nurturing him from this place of shared understanding even though they were physically far away.

After Dad moved to Rosen Springs, I visited once per week. With more frequent visits, less travel time to get to him, and fewer evenings away from home, each visit with Dad became a little lighter. Though the agenda was less packed, my visits remained focused around the logistics of daily life, much as they had been for the previous two years. They followed a predictable pattern: arrive, chat, attend to business, take a walk, eat lunch, depart. We did laundry, went to medical appointments, and painstakingly paid the bills together. Dad had always managed his finances with great care and attention. With the mechanical process of writing a check getting harder, we could spend thirty to forty-five minutes paying the phone bill. He acknowledged that he knew it didn't have to be that hard. If I offered to write a check for him, he would thank me, but ask that I help him instead. I talked him through each line, sometimes demonstrating how to shape a letter on a separate piece of paper. It was tedious for both of us, and sometimes frustrating for Dad, but it was so important to him to complete this process himself that he was willing to ask for help. Each time he got to the line where he added his signature, he could complete that part without prompting. It made me smile to see him sign with a flourish and we would both begin breathing more deeply again, suddenly aware of how tightly we had been holding our shoulders. I imagine that signing his name was a comforting act of self-affirmation that made the struggle of the whole check worthwhile. During these visits, I tried to normalize his new living situation. I would warm up soup for lunch, and we would eat in his apartment. We found something to attend to in each room of the small space and took walks around the complex. I was modeling the behaviors I hoped he would adopt as his own, still hopeful it would be possible for him to grow more comfortable in his surroundings. The community life at Rosen Springs was more valuable than any of my efforts though, providing a routine, and flow of people and daily activities. Within the predictable structure of the community, familiarity rather than adaptability ultimately facilitated settling in.

After the first few weeks, he didn't ask about the repairs to the condominium or returning to Connecticut. He was at ease in his apartment at Rosen Springs, and it had now become "the condo." He made friends with residents and eventually trusted the staff and routines. He had regular visits from me, Peter, and Matthew and periodic trips to our homes for holidays and events. For a year, things were smooth. As past and future continued to fade away in Dad's world, the essence of his being radiated brightly. Unencumbered by memory or anticipation and surrounded by caring community, he was blossoming. As I had always known him to be, he was kind and caring, attentive to others, gentle and deliberate in every action. He may not have always known me. He may not have recalled that he had traveled the world in his childhood, worked tirelessly in adulthood, and dreamed of a golden retirement. He may not have remembered the joys and challenges of raising four children and no longer understood the value in the stable life he had created for us. But he knew each moment and gave to it his earnest goodness.

Looking Closely

After a year in independent living, a few episodes raised safety concerns. First, Dad took a walk in the middle of the night. He had always been an avid walker, but he was becoming a wanderer and ended up outside very late. He eventually found his way back to the main entrance and rang the doorbell for reentry to the building. When the startled staff member let him in, she asked why he had been outside. He said that he had been looking for the bathroom. She brought him back to his apartment, took him to the bathroom, and tucked him into bed. There was no harm done, but the incident raised a small red flag. On another day, he might not have found his way back to the front door nor recognized it as familiar. It was also twenty degrees and icy that winter night. The next morning, he didn't have any recollection of having been out. When the head nurse called to tell me about it, I was paralyzed by this strange episode. I didn't know what it meant and wondered if I was supposed to intervene. If so, how? I didn't have to wonder long.

After a few days, Dad left the building in the middle of the night again but this time for a drive. Once more, by luck or by chance, he found his way back safely. But wandering by car was a gamble we could not allow to happen again. The staff at Rosen Springs recommended we intervene by taking Dad's car and moving him to the assisted living building where the doors were locked from the inside at 8 p.m. He might still get up for a walk in the middle of the night, but he would be limited to walking inside and would not be at risk of harming himself or anyone else.

My brothers and I had been debating his access to the car for a year. There was always the risk that he would go somewhere and not be able to get back home. As time wore on, we were also concerned that he would be driving and suddenly no longer know how to apply the rules of the road. This raised concerns not only for his safety but also for those around him. I made a point to continue to be his navigator and let him drive whenever I visited. His driving habits continued to be as cautious and precise as they always had been. Since moving to Rosen Springs, he had relied on me for every direction, including getting out of the parking lot. Even if we had driven the route dozens of times, the gaps in both retention and new thinking seemed to make everything unfamiliar all the time. I had felt certain that he knew his boundaries and would not risk getting lost or in a situation over his head. I had been sure that he never drove unless I was with him. But then he drove away that night, and it was clear I could not really be sure of anything.

I was surprised, relieved, and grateful Dad had made it back to Rosen Springs safely, frightened by what had happened, and anxious about the conversation I would have to have with him. For over a year we had all still been hoping that Dr. Berndt would initiate this conversation. But for whatever reason, Dr. Berndt either couldn't see or chose not to acknowledge any risks in Dad's life. He didn't pursue a medical evaluation or conversation to explore reasons why Dad should not live alone or continue to drive. Doctors regularly delve into other lifestyle factors and risks, and Dr. Berndt asked annually about firearms, drugs, and tobacco and alcohol use. He once described at length how a person will metabolize alcohol differently as he ages, but still neglected to discuss the ways a person might process information and stimulation differently over the same course of time. It had always seemed to me a cognitive evaluation to assess for elevated risks of living alone and driving could have been offered as simply and routinely as the annual blood screening that examined metabolic function. But those tests and conversations never happened, and I realized I had been looking for a scapegoat. I didn't want to be the bearer of bad news; I didn't want my own father to see me as someone who had taken away his liberty. Everything we did together was about safety, happiness, empowerment, and engagement. But it was time for me to stop hoping some authoritative word from the medical field would save me from initiating this conversation. I knew the staff at Rosen Springs had experience with these difficult situations and could help shape the conversation, but ultimately, I needed to take responsibility for the way it unfolded. I knew it was the right thing, but I hated having to do it.

The head nurse, the building manager, and I agreed to meet with Dad the next day to talk with him about what had happened. He had no recollection of his midnight drive and was once again frightened that he could have done something he did not recall. The nurse explained that something was happening in his brain. She assured him that he had not caused it and that he could not control it. She described what was happening as a little black spot on his brain covering up his ability to interpret information and make decisions. He was as white as a sheet, clearly unnerved by what she was describing. He was so cautious and so deliberate. Now he tried to absorb how, despite his best intentions, he could possibly have done something irrational and unsafe. Moreover, she was telling him he would continue to not be able to control this black spot's encroachment. She offered a referral to a neurologist who might be able to help figure out why it was happening and give us more information. Then, most importantly, she reassured him that he was in the right place and everyone at Rosen Springs would work together *and with him* to make sure he stayed safe. With that, he relaxed visibly and his color returned.

We all took a deep breath.

Then she added that part of staying safe would include giving me his car and moving to the assisted living building next door. He blanched again and turned to me. "What do you think?" he asked. I told him I thought it was the right thing to do and repeated the assurance that it was the best way for the people at Rosen Springs to support him in staying healthy and safe. I acknowledged that it probably sounded overwhelming and assured him I would take care of the logistics and make it as easy as possible. I suggested he might even feel relieved once he got settled. He asked, "But how will I get to the grocery store?" I had not anticipated that giving up the car would worry him more than moving. I explained to him that either the Rosen Springs driver or I could always take him anywhere he needed to go. But it really wasn't about the mode of transportation: his car was a symbol of independence. We went back and forth for a bit. Finally, I reminded him that every time he drove he had a responsibility to protect not only himself but everyone else on the road at that time. It was in the interest of protecting others that he should give up driving. He was still resistant, but this line of reasoning resonated with him. He practically threw the keys at me. "Fine. Take them," he growled. I thanked him and quickly put them in my pocket, hoping that by moving them out of sight I could remove his hurt too. I had the keys, but we had both been battered by the exchange.

By this time, we needed some fresh air. We thanked the nurse and building director for the conversation and went for a walk. Once outside, we talked lightly about the weather, the snow, my children. We filled the air with conversation about anything but the topic at hand, and the details of the morning's conversation dissipated in the clear winter sky though its weight hung heavily around us. When the sidewalk passed the assisted living building, we went in to warm up. The staff welcomed us kindly and offered us a tour. In many ways it mirrored the building he was in. We had a pleasant and comfortable visit. When we left, the receptionist asked if he would be moving in. He was surprised by the suggestion but responded, "We'll see." Though his tone was terse, I knew this was pretty close to acknowledgment and acceptance for Dad. We had an opening.

Back at his apartment, I made lunch. We watched television and chatted lightly. I was working hard to lift some of the weight hanging over our day. I had read that while someone with dementia may not remember the content of an experience with someone, they will retain the feeling of it. As we had forged this new relationship together over the last few years, I had kept this concept in mind day by day. It was especially important to me that I always left on a positive note, even when we had had challenging work or conversations during a visit. Surely the only feelings this day had evoked were loss, sadness, inadequacy, and trepidation. Dad sensed something looming but seemed unaware of exactly what was hanging over our heads. We managed to distract ourselves enough to eat lunch and equalize our moods. Eventually, I had to get home before Duncan and Thatcher got out of school.

As usual, when I was ready to leave, he wanted to walk me to the car. When I guided him through the parking lot to *his* car, he was confused. I replayed a shortened version of our earlier conversation including his consent that, for safety reasons, I would take his car with me. His face fell. Actually, his shoulders and chest fell too. He deflated in front of my eyes and turned away sadly. As I got into the car, I called after him softly, "I love you. I'll be back in a few days." My words sounded hollow in the wind. I was sure my actions were making too much discordant, hurtful noise for him to hear my spoken goodbye. I felt as if I had betrayed him, even though I knew that taking the car was the right thing to do. My only solace was that he would forget the cause of his sadness soon after I departed and, not long after, the sadness would dissipate too. As I drove away slowly, I looked in the rearview mirror to see Dad's friend Linda, who was returning from a walk, had stopped to wrap his slumped body in a hug. I wondered if he would be able to communicate why he was sad. In some way, maybe it didn't matter. Her hug and companionship would create space for happiness and ease to return. Soon they would be walking and talking together, and the mood of the day would fade as the evening unfolded.

Two years earlier, Dad had begun to say, "You're the boss" when he deferred a decision to me. He meant it kindly and I know he appreciated that I was taking some of the weight of decision making off of him, but I was very wary of the implication he was not his own boss. I had always deflected his declaration by lightheartedly joking back, "No, you are the boss. I am just bossy." As I drove away in Dad's car, I was aware that today I *had* been the boss. In the interest of his safety, I had pushed him to actions that were against his wishes. I could rationalize that it was time for him to relinquish some autonomy and independence. Living with tighter boundaries was not only appropriate, it was necessary. But by taking his car and approving the move to assisted living, I felt like I was stripping him of his personhood. Being the boss felt terrible.

When I returned a few days later, I was walking on eggshells. To my relief, I did not sense any lingering sadness or hint of resentment. While Dad never asked about his car, he curiously showed me the empty parking spot where he used to park it. While I waited somewhat impatiently for an assisted living apartment to become available, Dad seemed to forget all about it. Our visits returned to the same balance between taking care of business and taking pleasure in the simple joy of being together.

A few weeks later, after a successful Thanksgiving together, I wrote an email to my brothers and aunt to tell them about our holiday visit.

Subject: Dad's holiday visit

Hi All,

I wanted to share the good news of our Thanksgiving with Dad.

Thomas picked Dad up as a snowstorm arrived Wednesday afternoon, and they had an easy and comfortable drive despite the weather. Dad stayed with us Wednesday-Friday, and we enjoyed quiet conversations, lots of food, walks down the road, and watching the boys play in the snow. Dad particularly enjoyed watching the boys play chess, petting our dog, Karma, and quiet evening conversations. Matt and family came up to enliven Friday with energy, new topics of conversation, and drive Dad home. Dad clearly seemed to enjoy himself, but we were very careful to give him a lot of time and space to take care of his needs and a lot of support and direction so he never felt aimless. Thomas and I slept in the living room to provide middle of the night directions to the bathroom as needed. I think we all did a good job of meeting Dad where he is, and that helped us all enjoy the visit optimally. Our house was even able to sustain a level of heat that kept Dad comfortable!

One event that stands out to me as an indicator of where Dad is at this point in time was on Thursday afternoon. The boys and Thomas were outside, and I was beginning to prepare food. Thatcher had already counted out the silverware, and I asked Dad if he wanted to set the table. He was eager to help and picked up the silverware, but then looked from the table to the silverware in his hand and back to the table. He finally looked to me with a question in his eyes, and I offered to show him where the pieces belonged. We laid one place setting together. I carefully pointed out which piece went where and sometimes physically pointed out which utensil had which name. After the first setting was complete, he moved on to the next chair but hesitated again and looked over to me. We talked through each of the five place settings in exactly the same way. He could not even begin to replicate the pattern each time. It was second nature to stop what I was doing and support through the process, but after we were done I realized just how much support he needs and how many other daily basic functions might be becoming equally challenging. It was also a good reminder of how easy it is to provide him with opportunities to feel connected, helpful, and supported if we slow down enough to really notice where he is, how much he wants to offer, and what strengths still exist underneath the limitations.

So that was great. We know it's possible for Dad to enjoy being away for a few days still. Next time we will help him pack. He brought along some funny things and missed a few key items!

Lots of love,

Lisa

The week after Dad's Thanksgiving visit, I took him to the appointment with the neurologist. Dad fumbled his way through the health history with the nurse, looking to me for information and clarification on everything ranging from his address to the number of siblings and children he had. When the doctor arrived, he started to ask the same general personal history questions, then interrupted himself, saying, "Oh, I see it right here in the history. I have lots of notes." After reading through some of the electronic medical records (apparently he had notes from Dr. Berndt as well as Rosen Springs), the doctor looked straight at Dad and said, "You have dementia." He then turned to me and explained the five indicators of progressing dementia, what the notes told him about where dad might be (potentially between mild and moderate dementia), and what Dad's trajectory of decline might look like. He described a fairly consistent downward slope, like what I had been observing with Dad for a few years, and indicated that eventually people typically hit a steep decline. He described it as falling off a cliff.

It was pretty abrupt, and he was speaking only to me, as if Dad were not even there. Nothing he said about dementia was a surprise; I had seen so much change in Dad over an extended time. But his manner of talking about it so plainly and without apparent regard for how hard it might be for Dad to hear was unnerving. I was pretty taken aback. At one point, I looked to Dad and asked him if he was OK with hearing this assessment or surprised by any of it. He said he was OK and shook his head: he was not surprised. The doctor commended the recent decisions for Dad to stop driving and move to a higher level of care. When the neurologist described the benefits of the greater support at assisted living and the need to anticipate a narrowing scope of abilities, Dad protested, "I like to go outside and take my walks." The doctor responded reassuringly, "I share that goal with you. I want to minimize the need for you to make another move, and I want you to be safe, independent, and comfortable for as long as possible. I think by working together, we can help you have the freedom, comfort, and safety to continue to do as much as you wish for the longest possible amount of time." Dad seemed accepting, unfazed, and a little detached until the doctor said, "Well, let's do something about this." Dad enthusiastically responded, "OK!" The doctor requested blood work and a CT scan of the brain to begin ruling out easily identifiable possible causes of dementia, such as a tumor or a stroke. He also prescribed a rivastigmine patch, which would not reverse the progression of dementia or target any of the underlying causes of the symptoms, but it had been shown to stabilize brain function and slow the progressive decline.

The neurologist faced the reality of Dad's dementia with a no-nonsense, unapologetic, and confident approach. Either this approach or the progression of the dementia seemed to erase some of Dad's anxiety, self-awareness, shame, and embarrassment about his changing capacities and gave him an opportunity to be accepting. Maybe it also helped that I no longer arrived at Dad's medical appointments with my own anxieties, fears, or hopes already piqued. Either way, Dad was receptive to the doctor's initial assessment and responded to his recommendations with ease and levity. Later that day, back at "the condo" having lunch, Dad sat at the table facing out the living room window toward assisted living and memory care. Out of nowhere, he pointed to the building and said, "Well, we have the other building right there." He had processed some of the doctor's visit at a deeper level than I had previously thought. Over lunch, we talked for some time about the assisted living and memory care buildings and the continuity of care at Rosen Springs.

The patch that the neurologist prescribed created an opportunity to get Rosen Springs more involved. It needed to be replaced every twenty-four hours, a pattern that would have been hard for Dad to adopt on his own. He was amenable to having a nurse manage the patch application for him while he got used to it. Given that someone would be in his room daily, I told him I would also ask them to help more with the laundry too. He acknowledged that he was not doing a good job of keeping things clean. (He wore the same socks to the neurologist appointment that he had worn all three days he was at my house for Thanksgiving; they were easy to identify because they were mismatched.) Up to this point, in an effort to respect Dad's autonomy, the staff had backed off when he told them he didn't want them to take his laundry. As of that afternoon, he was amenable to some support, so I asked them to be more assertive about the laundry. For a few hours at least, Dad seemed to embrace the neurologist's assessment that additional support would help him sustain his current level of health, comfort, and relative independence.

Looking Around

A few weeks later, while I was on vacation, an apartment in assisted living opened up. Matthew took Dad out for lunch and a drive. While they were out, a moving crew took his belongings to the new apartment. When they got back to the complex and arrived at the new building, they had a very hard conversation. Dad was not happy, saying, "So this is how it's going to be." We had clearly undermined his self-determination. I felt guilty about not being there to support Dad with the transition and even more guilty to feel so relieved and grateful that it was Matthew's turn to be the bad guy. The room was a studio rather than a two bedroom, so it was instantly easier and more comfortable for Dad to navigate. By the time I visited two days later, he was fully settled in. In fact, he was unsure of what I meant when I asked about his "new place." He eventually told me that he was very happy where he was and asked me to promise him I would never make him move again. Of course, I couldn't promise that, but I told him how glad I was he was happy. He was insistent, but I could only assure him I would always stay by his side and make sure he was OK. I realized later that he may have actually been seeking my assurance that he would not lose any more capacity. I wouldn't have been able to promise that either, but perhaps it meant that he had a sense of the perceptual changes he was constantly negotiating.

In assisted living, with its increase in staff and routine, Dad had an open window for interpreting the world again despite his rapidly advancing dementia. With narrower boundaries, there were new opportunities for Dad to dwell more fully in the gifts and capacities he still had. Amidst the care and structure, he again blossomed. He walked many miles and participated in community service, yoga, Zumba, and ballroom dancing. At first glance, some of these activities were very out of character for Dad, the quiet, unassuming lawyer who had lived a fairly guarded life. The first time I saw him in Zumba class, full of joy and without a hint of inhibition, I couldn't hold back my delight and laughter. It was such a blessing for him to have this new lease on life. He was engaging with the world and people around him in new and surprising ways. The staff at Rosen Springs were able to approach Dad each day without expectation or history, and he was able to respond from the only place he had, the present moment. Even though I tried to be open to the unexpected, I am sure I still anticipated Dad's actions and behaviors based on who I knew him to be. And I am sure my expectations gave us guardrails that were supportive at some times and restrictive at other times. I am very sure it never would have occurred to me to bring him to a Zumba class.

Our relationship adjusted again in response to his new situation. When he moved to the assisted living building, I had his mail forwarded to my house and simply took care of business matters for him. In early April, he mentioned that he thought he might need to take care of his taxes. He had noticed other residents having tax conversations with their families and wondered if we should too. When I reminded him that we had completed his tax filing a few weeks earlier, he nodded gratefully and never brought up business or financial matters again.

My visits became opportunities for outings. We had long walks at the beach and in the woods. We observed the days we spent together very fully. In so doing, I closely observed the changing seasons, his changing condition, and our evolving connection. We had become closer than we had ever been before. He was a good father when I was young—honest, responsible, and loving with an easy and good-hearted laugh—but I did not have a sense of being close to him. He had worked long days and many weekends, so we didn't have a lot of shared time or experiences during my childhood. When I reached early adulthood, he patiently offered support, but I was busy asserting my independence. As I married and had children, he shared affection and appreciation for our growing family and was a steady and loving presence until dementia began to push him into isolation.

From time to time, I would dread my visits. The drive to Rosen Springs was eighty minutes, so I had a lot of time to wonder what mood Dad would be in, how much capacity he would have lost since the last time I had seen him, and if he would even know me. Possible scenarios played over and over in my head in a relentless game of "what-if." Inevitably, when I arrived, my worry would melt away. Our visits were not always easy or smooth, but he was usually happy to see me, grateful for my presence, and open to suggestions.

I eventually learned not to anticipate. My projections were futile and did not support me in being better prepared. The best way to be with Dad was to keep an open mind and open heart. It also helped to remain aware, flexible, and responsive. A lovely walk along the beach could become too cool and windy when we turned around to go back to the car. This had the potential to make an otherwise lovely afternoon stiff and cranky, but Dad would follow my mood and cues. If we pulled up our hoods and laughed at our predicament, we could arrive at the sun-warmed car breathless and giggling at our misadventure. I usually had a few chocolate chip cookies waiting for us there. The sweet treat offered a bit of self-indulgence that allowed our happiness to linger while we drove back up the road to Rosen Springs. I thought a lot about creating moments of joy in our time together. Each moment always felt incredibly fragile and at the same time heavy with the weight of its own importance.

Dad was completely unhinged from history, anticipation, and relationship. Whittled down to his core, he had simply expanded into himself. His profound goodness and kindness radiated through whatever mood, behavior, action, or inaction he presented. Beyond the damaged confines of his body and mind, his essence persisted unscathed.

After growing up in New England, I had moved west. I landed in a city with plenty of opportunities but still enough greenery for my rural roots. I was expanding my horizons without feeling completely untethered. I was employed doing meaningful work, interested in the community around me, running long distances, and maintaining strong friendships, but still I yearned for something different. I sensed I was not yet in my place, not yet doing what I was meant to do. One morning, sitting at a café with a friend, I noticed a sign for the first time.

Before enlightenment: Chop wood, carry water.
After enlightenment: Chop wood, carry water.

I had probably glanced over it a dozen times before, but on this particular morning, the sign practically screamed at me. The businesspeople, students, and young moms who frequented the place went about their business as usual—on computers and cell phones, reading newspapers, writing grocery lists, calming babies. It would have seemed a normal morning. My friend and I had been cherishing an hour of conversation carved out of our tight schedules and a sweet cinnamon roll indulgence carved out of our tight budgets. And then the sign completely captured my attention and held my imagination for months to come. It seemed to beckon to me to whittle my life down to its most fundamental. It suggested that there, in the most basic elements, I might find what was missing. Its offering grew in me until I was called to live its teaching.

My western exploration continued. There was nothing to prove or achieve, just a journey to be had. The road ahead was unfamiliar but not frightening. I was very simply seeking my place and following my inclinations where they led me. It seemed to me that "my place" would have a particular look, feel, and smell I would recognize as soon as I found it. I stopped wondering what I was supposed to *do*. I believed that I would recognize that too once I was in the right place.

That's how I got to Alaska and how I found Thomas along the trail. It's how we made a life there and then eventually found our way to Maine. Along the way we chopped wood and we carried water. In our little hand-made cabin off the grid, we embraced a simplicity that stripped life of pretense and invited new richness and possibilities. The lessons we gleaned from wilderness travel and simple living had probably been there all along, but there they were in plain sight. We worked hard and lived close to the earth. We made plans but adapted quickly when a situation called for change. We paid attention to each moment and learned from our experiences. We stayed together. We followed new paths as they arose. We trusted our instincts and relied on the interconnected wisdom of our hearts, bodies, and minds.

These same skills to adapt, to bond, to venture out on new, untraveled, and unmapped paths, and to rely on inner wisdom accompanied me while navigating the moments of joy and challenge that Dad and I met regularly.

The View from Here

Surprises and Gifts in Each Tender Moment

On backpacking trips in the mountains, our craving for perspective often governed the distance Thomas and I would travel each day. As we hiked into the afternoon, we would begin anticipating and looking for the ideal place to spend the night—a spot with water, flat land for the tent, and a view. This quest for a vista would typically bring us to a high spot where we could enjoy dinner with the camp set up a few hundred feet below. We would revel in the relief of shedding our packs, stretch our weary muscles, and soak up the vista while slowly pitching our tent and preparing our meal. We spent many late afternoons admiring mountains, valleys, and rivers from a vantage that allowed us a nearly 360-degree view of our surroundings. We could watch weather coming and going as we talked about our day's travel and contemplated the next day's route.

By the time dinner was ready, the sun would usually be low on the horizon and not offering much heat. As the wind picked up, we would rush to finish cooking and settle in to eat our meal with all of our layers on. Hoods up, we would crouch low to be out of the wind. And there at our feet, just beyond our soup bowls, would be delicate beauty. In our appreciation of the grandiose views and sunset, we would have neglected to notice the tiny lichen, moss, and wildflowers—the hardy life-forms that flourish on alpine rock, growing in tiny increments each year despite the challenges of wind and weather. They are a good reminder of persistence and tenacity, a call to remain strong despite challenges. The beauty of life is not just in the vast expanses; it is everywhere, including hiding in barely perceptible nooks and crannies. We can learn a lot by paying attention to what might not be readily seen or heard.

Vistas

A few months after moving Dad into assisted living, my brothers and I took him on a trip. For several years he had been waiting for the U.S. Open to be held in Tacoma, Washington. He had stored magazines, photos, and maps in a folder, eagerly anticipating the opportunity to attend the golf tournament under the shadow of Mount Rainier. He did not know it was finally around the corner. For that matter, he no longer knew or wondered about what was around any corner. He simply moved through each day, greeting each moment as it arose without anticipation or worry. He would not have known if the tournament came and went without him. But my brothers, aunt, and I would. We decided to make it happen for him. Everyone would stay with Aunt Julie and Uncle Ross at their home in Seattle, and we would spend one day at the golf course. We all deserved a bit of a vacation.

The staff at Rosen Springs were very supportive of the idea, believing that Dad would fully embrace a few days of vacation surrounded by family. They prepped his medications and prepped me for the amount of guidance and hands-on care he would need each day. They anticipated that with me by his side to guide him through carefully constructed days, he would be fine. Dad had been growing more erratic lately and was occasionally terse, anxious, and paranoid. He had also been up and wandering more at night. The nighttime wandering concerned us the most for our trip. We worried that if he walked around the house looking for something familiar, he could walk right out the door and into the street. To prevent that, Matthew would share a bedroom with Dad, and I would sleep on the couch just outside their door. Parenting had prepared us both to pay attention to middle of the night needs, and we knew that we could manage a few nights of broken sleep.

Matthew and I had been to Ross and Julie's home with Dad just two and a half years earlier and had hoped he would remember the house or at least feel comfortable there. Upon arriving, it was clear he did not remember it at all, but the view was instantly familiar to him. The commanding vista from their living room mirrored the one from his parents' old house. Looking out, he was both comforted and inspired by it. So was I. The waning summer snow on the peaks and glistening water prompted peaceful daydreaming and contentment. The expanse of the landscape was nurturing and relaxing while the hum of family conversation and laughter was invigorating.

We were careful to set up manageable and successful situations for Dad and scheduled our days with ample time to ensure we never felt rushed or stressed. Not surprisingly, transitions were the hardest: getting showered and dressed for the day, getting ready for bed, getting ready to leave the house. The staff at Rosen Springs had told me how much cuing they had been giving Dad around things like brushing teeth, showering, and dressing, but the prompts that had been sufficient in his own apartment were not enough in an unfamiliar space. However, with attention, kindness, laughter, and ample patience from both me and Dad, we fumbled through these activities each day with joy to spare.

It helped that over a year earlier, a few months after he moved into independent living, Dad and I had popped the bubble of self-consciousness that shrouds our bodies and their functions in embarrassment. We had returned to Connecticut for a surgical procedure with his urologist. The surgery was a success, but the anesthesia and post-op painkillers made his confusion complete for several days. He required hands-on assistance for everything, including the bathroom, shower, and eating. He was so adrift and malleable that his dependence was without self-awareness. In the process of attending to his immediate physical needs, my own self-awareness and timidity about imposing on his autonomy faded too. In those post-op days, I became a more competent and confident caregiver, and Dad became more willing to accept my support. Even as the medication-induced haze faded, it was clear we had replaced the increasingly fragile and dangerous construct of privacy with a circle of care, mutual respect, and acceptance. We quickly slipped into this familiar safe space during our weekend in Seattle.

Our trip to Washington was made extra special by the fact that it took place over Father's Day weekend. Dad was confused, but we stayed close and he stayed relaxed. The day we went to the course to watch the U.S. Open was sunny and warm, but not too warm. We walked a lot, avoided the crowds, and saw some favorite golfers up close.

We left the course before we got too tired. The golf was well played and so was our expedition. The next day, we stayed in, took a long walk along the beach, ordered takeout, and watched the final round on television at the house. A silly game of croquet in the backyard at sunset capped it all off. For a few days, Dad lived the joy-filled retirement of golf, family, and recreation we had all always envisioned.

We left early the next morning for the airport. As with the last three days, Dad was willing to go along with whatever we proposed, but he seemed confused. Through good-byes, navigating the airport, and the six-hour plane ride, he was flexible and good-natured, but quiet. Matthew's car was waiting for us at the airport garage, and then we began the two-hour car ride north. Matthew would drop Dad and me off at Rosen Springs and then proceed on to his house. I would help Dad settle in, and then Thomas would pick me up. We rode along the highway mostly in silence. I'm not sure if Matthew or I had begun talking about how fun the weekend had been or if Dad just sensed it was coming to a close, but I suddenly noticed tears were streaming down his face. He must have felt we were nearing the end of our trip. I offered tissues but words of solace seemed trivial. His silent tears were full of a deep and personal sorrow. He cried for most of the two-hour drive.

When we arrived, we got out of the car and hugged Matthew. As he drove away, Dad and I rang the doorbell. A staff member let us in and quietly welcomed Dad home. It was late and the halls were nearly empty. There were just a few staff around. I led the way to Dad's apartment. He followed me closely through the hallways, taking it all in. I was surprised to realize it was all unfamiliar to him again. We had only been away for a few days. For a moment, I worried we had shattered the carefully constructed balance of his routine by indulging in a once in a lifetime vacation he might not even remember.

When I opened the door to his apartment and walked in, he followed. He spun in a circle, looking around. Slowly, recognition crept in as he saw his corner cupboard, his table, his bookshelf, his artwork. At first, he was glad for the familiarity. "Oh, I recognize this. I've been here before," he said. Then his face fell as he remembered more. I can only guess that it was some uncomfortable and unhappy feeling of being there. Maybe he recalled frustration, isolation, loneliness, or confusion. He began to weep. "Am I going to stay here again? But it was so nice to be with everyone. That's the way it should be all the time. Why can't it be that way always?"

It was a great question without any good answers. There was no way to explain that the weekend we had just experienced together was a vacation. It was a moment out of time very carefully constructed to keep him healthy and happy. It had been wonderful and exhausting. Instead of trying to respond with words, I just hugged him and cried with him. Now, we were both sobbing. There was no way to explain that a disease had robbed him of his self-determination and self-expression. There was no way to explain that he couldn't live with his sister or his children. He would be miserable in our homes with the gentle chaos and unpredictability that accompany the lives of young families. So we just cried. Through his sobs, he asked if it would be this way forever. I told him, truthfully, that I did not know about forever. I just knew it was the right thing for now.

Fully consumed in a storm of emotions, we cried and hugged and hugged and cried. This was the closest he ever got to mourning the life no longer possible for him. Somehow, I managed to get his things unpacked and the suitcase put away. Maybe once it was all out of sight, he would forget about it, including his tremendous loss and this penetrating, aching sadness. I desperately wanted him to retain the joy of our trip and not the sorrow of returning home, but he was grieving.

We had been there for twenty minutes, and my phone kept ringing. Thomas was at the door waiting for me. I had hoped to get Dad relaxed and tucked into bed before I left, but when he realized I was not staying for the night, he was not about to settle in. Ever the gentleman, he insisted on putting his shoes back on and walking me down to the front door. There he gave Thomas a long, hard hug. Now all three of us were crying. Thomas and I had to explain again that we were leaving and he was staying. He was home now, and we had to get to our home where the boys were waiting for us. He did not understand. I nudged Dad's shoulders toward turning around so he could feel which direction he needed to go. He turned to look at the now unfamiliar place. "Go up the stairs. Your apartment is up the stairs. Get a good night's sleep." He nodded and, head down, moved to leave us. We watched from outside as he walked up the stairs. He didn't look back. I was grateful to know there were staff waiting at the top to greet him with a smile, and I hoped his sorrow left him as soon as he left us.

No longer trying to support Dad in his sadness, my own well of sorrow deepened as we drove away. I cried the whole way home. Again, my only solace was in the hope that Dad had quickly forgotten the weight of the encounter. After fretting for too long, I called Rosen Springs and asked the nurse to go check on him. She found him content in his room and helped him get ready for bed. Days later, if someone asked him about his family vacation to see the golf tournament, he would respond with joy and a sparkle in his eye. I was so relieved to know the enduring feeling was of the happiness we had fostered together. He never went back to that place of acute awareness of all he had lost or, if he did, it was not something he shared with me again. As his disease progressed and he withdrew deeper into himself, his waning self-awareness seemed to rob him of any further capacity to mourn his lost life.

The grief we experienced together that night while we sat on his bed hugging and holding each other was real and heavy. I was shaken for several days. We had touched the immeasurable loss and sorrow of his interrupted life in a place of deep awareness. I struggled with the paradox of mourning the loss of a person who was still living. It didn't seem right, yet I still mourned as a daughter who missed her father. I longed to see him nourished in his old age as he had provided nourishment for me and the others he had touched throughout his life. I wondered anew if we could have done it all another way. I cursed the busy lives and fragmented culture that keep us from honoring and integrating each generation's contribution into the fabric of our days. I would not touch this place of deep grief in myself again until the final weeks of Dad's life.

Ever so slowly, I peered out from beneath the shattering loss we had observed together to find that the joy, wisdom, and beauty that remained had just been polished. Barely perceptible wildflowers were blooming and they invited my attention.

The Flowers at Our Feet

Just two months after our trip, six months after the original move into assisted living, it was time for another move. Dad needed the extra staff support and structure of the memory care neighborhood. Verbal communication had become a greater challenge, and he was becoming confused and agitated more frequently. He had suggested to the staff that something was wrong, that he needed to make a change. It became clearer in his renewed struggle to navigate through each day and his increasing frustration. The staff talked to him about moving to the memory care wing, just around the corner from assisted living, and reported that he was reluctant but accepting. The dread and hesitation caused by anticipation had become familiar to all of us.

I took Dad for a walk at the beach so we could talk about it too. We began our conversation in the car on the way there. The weight of sadness and worry seemed to increase as we drove. The car was confining and mirrored the restrictions he worried were coming his way in the other building. He was already wearing a wander guard: an electronic bracelet that caused external doors to lock when he approached. The new building would not change that. The doors in memory care were locked for everyone. There would be more staff and structure to give him guidance and support as well as more opportunities to be active and engaged. I tried to appeal to the lawyer in him by rationally explaining that Rosen Springs had a legal responsibility to support residents at the appropriate level of care. The staff thought the extra personnel and more defined schedule in memory care would benefit him. We were talking in circles. My explanations did not address the worry and fear that accompanied a step into a new unknown. Dad, of course, could not see he was already dwelling in the unknown of his changing self.

When we arrived at the beach, we began walking and, as soon as we did, our conversation shifted. I finally answered his "why?" in a way that made sense. I reminded him of our second and final visit with the neurologist. After reviewing the blood work and CT scans, the neurologist had told Dad that his changing abilities were "nothing more than birthday candle disease, my friend." He had explained that he had signs of a "touch of dementia" and again described a slow but inevitable progression. The assertive, direct manner of our initial visit was replaced by a gentle sidestepping and shrug of the shoulders that told us we were on our own. He suggested we shift our focus to attentively responding to Dad's changing abilities in order to maximize his enjoyment of remaining capacities. I reminded Dad that when he encouraged us to be prepared to adapt, it was a time like this he had had in mind.

When we were leaving the neurologist's office after that second visit, I had been frustrated. After trying unsuccessfully to get Dr. Berndt to address our concerns just two years ago, we did not need to spend time with a doctor who trivialized them. We certainly did not need to spend time with anyone who belittled Dad's challenges or spoke about him as though he weren't there. In my anger, I held my tongue, and I am glad I did. Dad had been empowered and pushed to thoughtfulness by the man's monologue. As we drove away, he shared fragments of his thoughts: "*I knew something was wrong. He said I have Alzheimer's. There's a group that meets to talk about things like that. Maybe I'll go to one of their meetings, learn more . . .*" The doctor had not used the word Alzheimer's, but Dad had heard it. His own father had succumbed slowly to

Alzheimer's fifteen years earlier, and Dad may have long ago sensed that he was following in his footsteps. Maybe the word and concern that had been fluttering around in his mind had finally found a way to land. While I had been busy feeling offended by the doctor's dismissive bedside manner, Dad had heard what he needed to hear. His awareness that something was wrong had been validated by someone he deemed a respected authority.

Now at the beach, reminded of the neurologist's assessment and recommendations, Dad remembered them with surprising clarity. "I had forgotten about that. I didn't want to hear it, so I stuffed it way back in my head under some newspapers and then I stomped on it to keep it down for good measure." He mimed with his hands to show me how he had folded up this piece of information, placed it on the ground, piled newspapers on it, and then stomped on it. He hadn't wanted to face it at the time, so he had put it far away and then forgotten about it. He explained that he had known that something was not right and had just been trying to go about his business while also struggling to keep it all together. Now, he was relieved to be reminded there was a reality beyond his control that was the cause of his struggle. He was living with dementia. He thanked me genuinely for bringing it up and naming it again. His renewed awareness seemed to relieve him of the need to hold all of the fragments of his world together by himself. With the wide view to the ocean and the fresh air in our lungs, we cleared a few cobwebs and regained some lightness and joy as we walked and talked at the beach that day.

When moving day came, Rosen Springs took care of it all. Dad hardly seemed to notice that, after the morning's outing, he returned to a different room in a different portion of the building. When the manager from assisted living stopped by the next day to see how he was "settling into his new room," he said, "What new room? I've always been here," and closed the door on her. The move to memory care was almost without transition. I was intrigued by this renewed capacity to absorb a change in environment. Settling into his first apartment at Rosen Springs a year and a half earlier had been so full of stress and effort. Finding the front door, bathroom, and dining room were struggles. At that time, he was still relying on his faltering memory and trying to create routines that would guide him through daily functions. By the time he moved to assisted living and then memory care, he did not—and could not—rely on his memory at all. He looked to the world around him for clues every minute of every day. Each time he moved to a different level of care, the increased staffing and activity in each environment provided more of the clues that allowed him to function fully. A staff member would listen for sounds of stirring in his room in the morning. As soon as he was awake, she would step in to provide gentle prompts for morning routines. At any time of day or night, he could open his door, walk into the hallway, and keep walking until he found a person or activity. His ability to orient himself in time and place seemed to renew a sense of safety and security. True to Maslow's hierarchy—the theory that when basic needs are met a person is open to self-actualization—Dad's pathway to his potential was reestablished.

I observed this positive impact of each move after it happened, but I worried about each one too. I hated confronting Dad's declining abilities by imposing a "solution." Yet each new setting proved to meet his current needs better than his previous environment had and, importantly, left room for inevitable upcoming changes.

In memory care, Dad found new ways to provide support, encouragement, and joy to the staff and residents with whom he shared his days. He was helpful, generous, and kind as always. He developed a special friendship with a woman who enjoyed walking as much as he did, and they would walk lap after lap through the building. When they tired, they would sit down together and wordlessly hold hands while the time passed. He enjoyed showering her with care and attention, and she soaked it up. I talked with my brothers and with the Rosen Springs staff about the relationship, mutuality, and what consent looks like among two adults whose decision making is compromised. In the end, it became an opportunity for us to again notice how much of Dad's core self remained and how persistently it expressed itself. As Peter observed, "Dad has always had so much love to give." Even as his physical and intellectual capacities continued to diminish, he was finding new ways to share that love with others.

The care staff and medical team at Rosen Springs did the hard work of pulling in closer when necessary to ensure that his basic needs were met and Dad engaged in each day as fully as he desired. I regained the ability to simply be with him, attentive to the offerings and situations that might bring him joy or serenity. We continued to spend a lot of time walking and a lot of time at the beach. Our favorite outing was to stop by a deli, pick up a few sandwiches and drinks, and take them to the beach. If it was cold, we had a picnic in the car, watching the waves and clouds while we ate. When it was warm, we could eat in the company of seagulls on a bench and then walk the long boardwalk as far as we dared.

There was a quality of being with Dad during this time that fostered a deepening connection. Knowing that each moment was only itself—no more and no less than a blink in time—liberated it in profound ways. Without the pretense of creating memory or paving a path to the future, each moment could simply be. Our conversations became very simple and topical. Our words often dwindled into silence. Occasionally, Dad initiated conversations out of the silence by asking the benign question "So, what have you been up to?" I would answer and then we would fall into silence for a bit. Then he would ask again, "So, what have you been up to?" I would answer again. Each time he asked, he was completely unaware of having had this conversation already so I would answer with something new. As I answered this question each time, it became like a peeling away of the layers of my life. I would share the most topical mundane life events first: "I drove the carpool yesterday. We've been eating asparagus from the garden. I am reading an interesting book. Next weekend we are planning to . . ." With each repetition, I would offer an answer that progressively dug into the roots of something more important to me. If he asked enough times, I would often offer up an unresolved problem: "I have an interesting new project. I've been trying to decide between . . . I've been wondering about . . ."

Periodically, once I had gotten past the mundane reporting and into the complex wonderings, instead of asking his question again, he would respond with a relevant insight or observation. A few times, he offered such astute, clear commentary that, for a while, I found myself baiting our conversations to see if he would grant me another nugget of wisdom. I wanted to soak up the intelligence and awareness that his narrowing understanding of the world was offering to him. He thoughtfully examined questions and problems from his unique perspective and encouraged patient acceptance over hasty resolution. I told him about an interesting project I had started for a local organization and how I was worried about whether or not they would be able to sustain it after I stepped away. He said, "Well, you'll check on it from time to time." I took his advice and proposed an ongoing contract to the program manager that would evaluate the work we had started; she was thrilled with the idea. It had not even occurred to me to build in continuing support for this project, but it was obvious to Dad. He had always been slow, steady, and methodical, but now that his body was mirroring his mindset, his deliberate nature took on the quality of an art form. I was attentive to observing and learning from him.

For a while, we found a balance in our conversations that gave him the space and authority to share the wisdom of an elder. I began to cry when I told Dad how happy I was that Duncan, my older son, was going to boarding school in the fall but also how much I would miss him. Dad just said, "It *will* be hard for you. It *will* be OK," and leaned in to give me a comforting kiss on the cheek. I began to cry harder, but deep joy shone through my tears as I recognized Dad's radiant love and care. I had been so busy trying to support him in feeling safe and cared for that I was only offering my competence. Now, when I offered him my vulnerability, a room opened for him to offer me *his* competence and care again. With close attention to what was not easily seen or heard, I could still feel and touch his intelligence, honesty, and love.

The Edge of the Cliff

Eventually, interpreting my words became too much work. Instead of bringing us closer, conversation began to frustrate Dad. In the discomfort, sometimes I would keep rambling, almost as if to console myself. When I quieted, I would notice I had been maintaining a monologue that had the effect of keeping my companion shut out. When we simply held hands and appreciated being together, we were connected and pleasantly aware of one another and our surroundings.

As Dad expressed himself less verbally, I began to seek ways to keep him happy and healthy in his body. He was already engaging as fully as possible in activities at Rosen Springs. Physical therapy provided periodic support for safe physical engagement and developed strategies for support that kept Dad in charge of the basic activities of daily living as long as possible. Nonetheless, he seemed to be getting slower and stiffer by the day. I wondered if massage would help and found a massage therapist who was willing to give it a try. We approached the first visit as an experiment. It was likely that Dad had never had a massage before, and I was not sure how he would respond. As with most things we had endeavored, he was willing to go along. I led him through each step with words and guiding touch. Sit in this chair. Take off your shoes. Walk over to this table. Step up on the stool. Sit down on the table. Take off your shirt and belt. Lie down on this table so your head is facing down. Getting onto the massage table was a physical and mental stretch, but it was worth it. Thirty minutes later, he emerged deeply relaxed and grateful.

We returned every two weeks, and our visits became familiar. He would respond as soon as we walked into the massage studio. His shoulders would relax and his smile would widen, feeling the serenity in the space and perhaps anticipating in his body the soothing moments that were to come. So little was familiar in his world from one moment to the next, but his body seemed to recognize and respond to the peace and connection in that space. Over those months, I am certain that the positive affirmation of the massage therapist's voice, the touch of her hands, and her loving attention allowed him to find moments of comfort and peace not otherwise attainable. He could no longer reason or walk his way to contentment but, during each visit, the massage therapist ushered his body, mind, and heart into alignment and he could rest there. It was a welcome respite.

At the same time that Dad began massage, I began to take yoga classes. I had participated in yoga periodically throughout much of my adult life, but I had never been consistent about it. This time, I became hooked on the routine of attending a weekly class and dove into the discipline of a regular practice after the first class. Perhaps I was getting through yoga what Dad was getting through massage. I eagerly welcomed the opportunity to quiet my mind and align it with my heart. I observed the flexibility and strength building in my body while the stability and rhythm of the asanas quieted my thoughts and soothed my emotions.

Dad's emotions became more volatile as he became less verbal. I began to get phone calls from Rosen Springs about unsafe behavior. When frustrated or confused, Dad reacted aggressively toward staff and sometimes residents. The first few times this happened, he was sent to the emergency room for a determination of whether his aggressive behavior was caused by infection or if it represented a transition to a new normal. The first time, I rushed down to be with him at the hospital. It was, like any ER visit, more waiting than evaluation. I arrived to find him resting on a bed in front of the nurses' station. He was relaxed and content, albeit more confused than ever by the bustling activity around him and the sedative they had given him when they picked him up. I stayed with him for several hours as they evaluated blood work and a urine sample. When they finally discharged him, he had a prescription for an anti-anxiety medication to "get through the weekend."

After he was discharged, I took him back to Rosen Springs. We had missed their dinner hour, but there hadn't been dessert with the hospital meal so we sat down in the dining room for a bowl of ice cream. Dad kissed and hugged the young care provider who brought it to him and told her how much he loved her. As I fed him small spoonfuls of vanilla ice cream, he cried and told me repeatedly how sorry he was to be so much trouble. I assured him that he was not any trouble at all and I was sorry he had to spend the afternoon and evening in the ER. Bits of conversation rose and fell amid the tears, and the ice cream melted faster than he could eat it. I would have helped him eat it, but I had a huge lump in my throat. When the remaining ice cream was a warming soupy mess, I walked him to his room, and he let me help him into pajamas. I tucked him into bed and left him with a kiss on the forehead. A lot had changed since I had tried to settle him in for bedtime after our golf vacation almost a year earlier.

Whenever I felt regret after a visit with Dad, I wrote him letters that I knew he would never read. They bridged the gap between what I had said and what I wished I could say. Sometimes the words remained unspoken because I simply didn't think fast enough in each moment to be both present and reflective. Sometimes the words hadn't been spoken because I knew he wouldn't understand the meaning in them. The letters lightened the regret and sadness I carried and gave me back the adaptability required to be fully present within the time we had together.

Dear Dad,

There are so many things I needed to tell you today, but they got stuck in my heart or stuck in my throat. Each time I see you, I walk away wishing that I could do something to alleviate your situation. I can't, nor can you. The problems, behaviors, medications, doctors' visits, living situation, all of it, were not your intention. You did not bring this upon yourself, nor can you will, work, or imagine it away. I wish you could know that deep in your heart. Maybe it would make you less frustrated and less sad.

Here's the good news. The changes in your brain have changed the way you live your life, but they have not changed you. I still know who you are. It's as clear as a blue sky day. You are my moral compass. You are a gentleman. I used to tease you about your halo's shine. It remains as bright now as it was when you were in control of your actions. You are kind, concerned for others, and selfless. Even now as you struggle to find your way from minute to minute and day to day, your attention is outward to those around you and how you can make their moments better. The confusion that has fallen upon you and caused the world to shift is only a cloak that masks your true intentions and creates an obstacle to clear seeing and easy motion.

Know this deep in your heart. You are good and kind. You have done so much good for so many people and have shaped others through your example. It seems so unjust that you should suffer in this way. You are handling it with grace and strength. Still, I wish I could lift that suffering from you. It is hard to know that you are hurting and cannot understand why. In my helplessness, I am left only with hope that you feel held and nurtured by a grace that is beyond our reach.

I love you.

We had hit the point that the neurologist had described as "falling off a cliff." It was an unpleasant analogy that I had not spent much time thinking about. He had described the likely progression of dementia as slow and methodical for a time until, inevitably, there would be this steep decline. As I received more phone calls about ER visits, rapidly changing behavior, and increasing physical needs, I recognized that Dad was teetering at the edge of the cliff.

By this time, Dad was under the care of a geriatric psychiatrist, Dr. Max, who had managed to stabilize his moods and anxiety fairly well. Dr. Max explained that it is not uncommon to find depression or anxiety accompanying dementia. That struck me as completely logical. Of course, anxiety will increase if each new moment arises as a surprise. Of course, depression will crop up if there is an awareness of declining capacity, especially if it cannot be articulated or understood. I wondered why we hadn't learned this sooner but was mostly grateful he was identifying and treating these partner problems now. Most importantly, this doctor was caring and compassionate. Though Dad met Dr. Max anew each visit, he greatly enjoyed the introduction each time. Dad's responses were often inarticulate and rambling, but Dr. Max's combination of talk therapy and moderate medication management provided a new level of validation and humanity that both Dad and I appreciated.

I never witnessed the aggressive behavior that caused Dad to visit the ER a half dozen times over the course of that summer. Dr. Max and Rosen Springs carefully monitored the frequency and intensity of these episodes and attempted to manage his anxiety medications in a way that would keep Dad in equilibrium rather than bouncing between extremes. Dr. Max was very intentional about using the medication to mitigate emotional response in order to avoid undesirable behavior, but he did not want to rob Dad of potential positive emotions in the process. I visualized the medications as having the potential to dampen the ends of Dad's emotional spectrum—his positive emotions as well as his negative ones. With Dad's experience of the world already so limited, I appreciated Dr. Max's careful approach yet I also worried a lot about the possibility that someone would be hurt during an episode of aggression. To his core, Dad would never wish to hurt anyone, and I desperately wanted to protect him from the possibility he could violate his own values. The staff understood and respected that Dad's outbursts were caused by confusion, and they were careful to protect themselves and others if an interaction was spiraling out of control. When I worried that Dad's behavior would push him out of the range of care that Rosen Springs could provide, they assured me their residential care and medical teams would work closely with Dr. Max to "try everything possible to make sure that would not happen."

Dad required more and more attention from the staff at Rosen Springs. I spent more and more time on the phone negotiating recommendations from ER visits, Dr. Max, and Rosen Springs's medical team and physical therapy. My responsibilities were shifting once again. While I was not providing the daily care, I felt responsible for ensuring all of the pieces were working together to give Dad what he needed for health and happiness. Over the years I had dedicated myself to caregiving, I had grown to recognize the reciprocity and mutual benefit of our relationship and my attachment to it. I was not only deeply committed to providing him with the care and attention of others, I was devoted to offering as much of my time, love, and companionship as possible.

Subject: an update

Hi All,

I have been getting a lot of phone calls from Rosen Springs about incidents of agitation and aggression. Sometimes there are one or two per week. Sometimes it feels daily. I am concerned that Dad is getting to these places of excessive agitation and aggression so often. I imagine it doesn't feel good to him, but I also am worried for the safety of the other residents and care managers. His aggression is usually focused at someone and sounds adrenaline-filled. So far no one has been hurt, but I imagine that people are beginning to not feel safe around Dad. I will call a few agencies to see about hiring a personal companion to visit a few times per week. It seems like additional support or attention in the late afternoon/evening could be helpful. I have never seen Dad get to a heightened state of stress or agitation, but I usually visit in the morning and leave him by 2 p.m. He does seem to be getting tired and withdrawn by then, but not agitated.

I have noticed that Dad has slowed remarkably. He seems very unsure of his body's place in the world—unsure that the ground or a chair will support him. It's hard to tell whether his vision is changing and he can't see well or if his mind is not interpreting what his eyes are seeing. In either case, depth perception is definitely distorted. Last week, we went to the park and he was tired by the walk from the parking lot into the field. We started to step onto the trail, and then I looked at his face, noticed how hard he was working and suggested we turn around. We sat on a bench to rest twice on our way back to the car.

I shared these observations with Rosen Springs and asked that the care staff give him a little more time for physical activities. Maybe that will help decrease his agitation too.

I will keep you posted about my conversations later this week and my visit with Dad on Friday. Send him your calm and peaceful thoughts.

Love,

Lisa

I continued to visit weekly, but our walks had become shorter and shorter. Dad was unsteady and seemed to tire easily. He withdrew deeper into himself. Over those months, I came to enjoy a stillness within Dad and within myself. I relied on his facial expressions, posture, and reflexive movement to show me how he felt about an environment or a situation. He sensed when I was tense or watching the time. If I were worried about getting back home in time to pick up the boys from school, he would become agitated. His emotional state mirrored mine. I learned to still my mind and energy when I was with him in order to protect the sanctity of our time together. I learned to be quiet and to be in communion with him in that hush. When we were at the beach, he would follow my gaze to the horizon. We would laugh together at the opportunistic seagulls at our feet waiting for one of us to drop a bite of sandwich. A few times, we visited an old stone seaside chapel. The doors were often open, and we could take refuge from the summer sun in the cool, dark, and sacred space. Once, we sat in the front pew as the organist practiced and Dad hummed along reverently with the wordless notes for half an hour. These days taught me to protect space for unspoken meaning and the beauty that could arise at any moment. There was a quality of deep intention in our time together that not only enriched our relationship but also showed me a vision of my best self. All of my relationships and activities were worthy of this level of attention.

⁓

During my first summer in Alaska, I camped in a scree field at the edge of a glacier. The crew of high school volunteers I led was building a few sections of trail through the rocky terrain that had emerged at the sides of a receding glacier. We were tasked with building a rock bridge and causeway that would withstand time and water and keep hikers safely on the trail. The trail paralleled the glacier, following contours of rock and water exposed as the mass of ice slowly melted. Our camp was tucked into a basin between the trail and the massive, ancient hunk of ice and earth that served as both our guardian and our tormenter. The microclimate created by the merging of glacier and sky was cool and moist. When it wasn't raining, the fog was thick. If the fog lifted near midday, the sun was warm, but if the wind was blowing down the glacier, it carried the coolness of the ice with it. I often felt chilled to the bone beneath the warmth of my exertion that summer.

One night, a strong storm came in from across the mountains on the other side of the trail. We rushed to finish dinner and cleanup chores and hastily retreated to our tents. It was hard to stand against the force of wind and nearly impossible to hear one another above its howl. Isolated in my tent, I felt protected from the fierceness of the wind but anxious about being separated from the students. They would look out for one another and would lie low while the storm passed. There wasn't lightning, so we just had to stay hunkered down from the wind and the eventual deluge of rain. I sat in the middle of my tent and tried to write in my journal. Every few gusts, the wall of the tent would bow and hit me on the cheek. After a few thumps, I felt like I was in a comedy routine. I was sitting blithely in the middle of the storm trying to write my mundane reflections on the day while the wind commanded me to pay attention to the present moment. With one big gust, the tent wall folded in and created momentum that pulled the whole structure over, taking me with it scrambling like a hamster in a ball. I shrieked with surprise and envisioned the tent, with me in it, rolling like a tumbleweed into the glacier below us. I spread out as wide as I could, trying to take up space and distribute my weight to the corners.

Two of the students had heard my yelp and came running. They helped me right the tent and we staked it out again as well as we could in the rocky field. As they returned to their tent, bent low against the wind, I got back into mine, newly reminded of my vulnerability in this wilderness. I lay sleepless for several hours that night, frail and unsure about how to live in a world that changes in an instant over and over again. The rock that we worked with daily and the glacier that loomed nearby hinted at permanence, but even they change. Rocks can be broken. The glacier is melting. Tomorrow will never be the same as today.

Eventually, I fell into sleep and, at some point in the night, the wind subsided. In the thick fog of the still morning and in the company of steaming oatmeal and the entire crew, my rescuers and I recounted the story of the tumbleweed tent with laughter and levity. Less ominous now in the light of day, we embraced our awareness that life is big and unpredictable. We are not in charge. Our comfort rests in our ability to give and receive support and care. Our strength builds from our willingness to adapt to changing circumstances and the ever-changing landscape.

~

As the decline in Dad's physical capacity accelerated, our family had been thinking carefully about the future and preparing for some major transitions. Thomas, Duncan, Thatcher, and I needed to stretch and grow in new directions, and that required rebalancing caregiving with family needs. For the upcoming school year, we would live and work on two separate continents. I would travel between the two, providing consistency and a bridge between both worlds. Thomas would be working in Dubai and our younger son, Thatcher, would attend school there. Duncan would attend boarding school in New England. I would spend some of the year in Dubai and travel back monthly to spend time with Dad and be with Duncan during his school vacations. While it meant that I would no longer be able to visit Dad weekly, during the weeks I was home I could visit more often. We thought carefully through the give-and-take this arrangement would require for all members of the family and agreed we would make it work. I welcomed the sense of possibility inherent in exploring a new culture and landscape in Dubai and knew that the outward exploration would be positive for all of us. At the same time, I found myself deep in relationship with Dad, mirroring his retreat inward and drawn to the comfort and familiarity of our life at home.

☙ 4 ❧

Journey's End

Settling In and Bearing Witness

Absorbed by the unmapped wilderness of mind and heart with Dad, I was glad for the familiarity and well-worn patterns of our Maine landscape. In Alaska, we had cleared only small swatches of open space out of the forest. We had a parking spot by the road, a trail to the small clearing where we built the cabin, and a trail extending to the outhouse nestled in the thicket a dozen yards farther in. The rest of the land remained thick with highbush cranberry and birch, cottonwood, and spruce trees. We were reluctant to impose our humanity on the wild space and tried to live inconspicuously. Humans had likely moved through this area before, but none had ever stayed long. We also saw ourselves as temporary visitors, not residents.

When we moved to Maine, we settled in an old farm-house in the middle of a field that had once been cattle forage. This was land that had been occupied, altered, and actively managed by humans for generations. Evidence of past long-term inhabitants was everywhere we looked. The stories of human occupation and imposition were told in the clear-cuts, logging trails, and stone walls in the forest surrounding the field. A creek flowed along-side the house, through the field, and into the forest. A few hundred yards down the drainage, it opened into a wide pool. We imagined that at one point the creek had been dammed to create a water hole for the cattle. By the time we arrived, the dam had long been breached and the pool was now a wide circle of mud, a perfect spot for play. When they were young, Duncan and Thatcher spent hours breaking natural dams we found along the creek and building new dams when they felt inclined to make a diversion. We caught newts in one spot and harvested clay from the bank in another. There was so much human history already here that we readily wrote ourselves into the landscape's evolving story.

We cleared some trees to enhance the view to the east and built raised beds for our garden. We offered a portion of the field to farmers who were seeking more space to grow food for the local market. We fixed up the old farmhouse, exposing old timbers and adding enough windows to bring the outdoors in. We grew deep roots on this patch of land and in the community. Amid the distractions offered by school, work, conferences, com-munity commitments, caregiving, and soccer practices, Thomas and I continued to live by the principles of sim-ple living we had learned in the wilderness. While we no longer hauled our water, we continued to chop wood among dozens of other daily indoor and outdoor chores. We lived with attention and intention, responsive to opportunities and needs as they arose.

I leaned into the security of our land more fully as Dad neared the end of his life. I remained determined to keep him company on this unknown and lonely path, but while dementia had completely uprooted Dad, I felt literally grounded. I watched the sun rise over our fields in the early morning. In the evening, I sat by the wood-stove waiting for the moon to come up. The expansive view to the horizon and the rhythm of life on our small farm were reassuring counterweights to the unfamiliar experience unfolding as Dad's decline accelerated.

A Change of Direction

Early in the fall, the ER visits became more frequent. Dad had begun to fall. Anytime he was found on the floor, he needed to be evaluated at the ER to be sure he hadn't injured anything as he hit the ground. It was rare for a week to pass without an incident. His limbs were no longer responding to his brain. Or maybe his brain was no longer sending the proper messages to his limbs. Or maybe his legs simply were not strong enough to hold him. I had seen signs of this coming when I tried to help him onto the massage table or in and out of the car. He would look at the car seat as if he were unsure how to get from standing next to it to sitting in it. I would point at his left foot and say, "Lift that one up." He would look at me and then at his foot on the ground incredulously. I was suggesting something impossible. If I pulled on his pant cuff to start the motion, he would lift his foot into the car and the rest of his body followed. Our time together over the summer was full of these moments of support. I hadn't recognized them as a foreshadowing until his physical problems began to cascade.

When I left for Dubai in the second week of September, I was worried about being away. Dad had been in memory care for a year, and the staff there had become familiar, truly like family, to both him and me. I was confident my relationship with the staff was strong enough that we could manage any adjustments to care over the phone. I rationalized that I couldn't do much more than that anyway. But Dad's condition had been changing so rapidly over the last few months. I told myself my weekly visits had become more for me than they were for him. I still wanted to be a frequent companion, but I could no longer tell how much my presence supported him. I tried to convince myself the separation was OK, but it was extremely hard to be away; it was not possible to rationalize away my heartache.

When I returned to Maine three weeks later, Dad had another ER visit. It was his last. At this point, the ER was not going to find any conditions we would treat. Dad's body was clearly beginning to shut down, and any intervention that interrupted that process would only prolong his suffering. Each visit to the hospital was exhausting and disorienting for him and failed to offer any insight for his care team about how best to provide comfort. Long before dementia had settled in, Dad and I had talked about the role he saw for medical intervention in end of life care. I knew he did not want to have his life maintained or prolonged medically. He had completed an advance directive that stated his end of life wishes, but we had also talked at length about subtler aspects of medical intervention. He was clear about wanting to live and die as naturally and comfortably as possible. When I explained this to the staff at Rosen Springs, they suggested I meet with hospice to learn about a different approach to care.

I extended my visit to the States for a few more days so that I could enroll Dad in hospice care and get to know their team a bit. The hospice's focus on providing comfort rather than seeking to identify and treat pathology was a huge relief. Their engagement shifted how the staff at Rosen Springs approached Dad's care. It was a partnership I should have sought out months earlier, but I didn't know to want it. I had often been grateful for the careful financial planning that had allowed us to make decisions for my Dad's care based on his needs without worrying about costs. He had planned well for his future. Now I was grateful for the long conversations we had had many years earlier about medical care, life, and death. He could not communicate his wishes anymore, but I was confident I could advocate on his behalf in the same way he would have advocated for himself. Hospice got Dad a mechanical lift and a comfortable wheelchair so that he could be up and out of bed comfortably when he was awake. They worked with the care staff to adjust schedules and expectations so that the combination of rest, nutrition, and stimulation in each day adapted to his rapidly changing needs. No new rhythm remained in place for long.

When I got back to Dubai, I was terribly restless. I did not like being unable to reconcile the reports I received from Rosen Springs and hospice with my own observations. I struggled with the mixed emotions of both wanting to be with Dad and fearing that if I were with him I wouldn't do or say the right thing. I was afraid I would get in the way if I were there, yet it also felt like the wrong time to be so far away. After spending the last few years getting close and building a strong and trusting relationship, had I abandoned Dad just when he needed my companionship the most? We were over ten thousand miles apart and his body was winding down while mine became increasingly fretful and anxious. I knew that even if I were in Maine I wouldn't be able to be with him all the time. I trusted the staff at Rosen Springs to provide exceptional physical and emotional care, but I wanted to be there too. In my restlessness, I paced, wrote, cleaned, walked—and I watched the sky.

The previous summer, Dad and I had stood outside together. We had been to a massage appointment and a picnic at the beach that morning. I had grown accustomed to him not being chatty, but that day he had seemed deep in thought. As we walked toward the building, Dad stopped and turned away from the door, leaning on a railing and looking up at the sky. He stood gazing somewhat longingly into a place that I could not see. The sky was crystal clear blue. There were no clouds, no birds, none of the contrails he so enjoyed noticing. A breeze blew so gently it didn't rustle the leaves in the trees. Dad seemed to be looking beyond where the eye could reach. I waited and watched him for a few minutes. Finally I said, "You look like you want to be up there. We have to go inside now, but we can let the wind carry our spirits away." He looked at me with deep gratitude, and we shared a hug. I must have given words to some unspoken thoughts. Now I wondered if perhaps he had already offered his spirit to the wind and was just waiting patiently for his body to release its tight grip on life.

When I returned to Maine in early November, I planned to stay. There wasn't much I could do besides keep him company, bear witness, and continue to show up. Even after all we had been through, I didn't know what else to do. I just knew I needed to be present. It would have to be enough.

A Moment of Grace

I arranged for the hospice chaplain to offer my Dad the Sacrament of the Sick. In his early adulthood, Dad had been a member of the vestry at our church. I hoped that the words of the sacrament would bring him solace, and I wondered if they would help his body, mind, and spirit to unify in a recognition that his dying process had begun. When Dad had started to decline, we never discussed the inevitable progression of disease. Nobody had ever explained that his condition was terminal and his body's systems would close down one at a time until he died. In the early years, it was clear enough that memory, reasoning, emotional regulation, and verbal capacity were waning, but those were our only focus. We never discussed that other abilities we take for granted would fade away too. Standing up, walking, chewing, and swallowing would become challenging and then impossible. None of the doctors we had met along the way had prepared him or me for this. Perhaps it would have been too much for him to process with the limited mental reasoning he had left. Nonetheless, it felt unfair that, after years of suffering with a terminal illness, he should arrive at his dying without any opportunity for spiritual or emotional preparation. If there were regrets, gratitude, longings, or concerns, he would not have had the opening in a conversation to communicate them. I had never considered looking beyond the medical or residential care community for information or resources. I had listened to a CD of Frank Ostaseski's *Being a Compassionate Companion* a year earlier (twice, no less). At the time, it made more sense to apply the teachings to being a compassionate companion for Dad's living. Now that we had arrived at his dying, I was grateful to have had the introduction. I was also grateful for the layers of support that hospice offered both Dad and me generously and competently.

Since Dad had been mostly nonverbal for a few months, he could not tell us how he felt or what he was experiencing. If he spoke at all, the words were mumbled or whispered. He was often lightly asleep in his wheelchair when I arrived for a visit. Sometimes he would acknowledge my presence with a nod or smile when I said hello and gave him a hug. He was unable to hold his head up, so his chin rested on his chest; even if his eyes opened, he could only see me if I brought my face down to his chest to be in his visual range. Sometimes he would remain drifting after my greeting. If he was awake, he was usually very restless, tugging at the corners of a blanket or pillow. He seemed uncomfortable in his skin. On those days, he received heavier doses of morphine and lorazepam to control pain and anxiety. We did not know the source of discomfort he was expressing, but the medical team was sure that he was in pain by the way his body responded to the medication. When he received it, his fidgeting would subside and the deep creases across his eyebrows and forehead would soften. His body would relax and, often, he would drift into sleep.

The day that the chaplain was scheduled to come for the Sacrament of the Sick, Dad was surprisingly alert and chatty. The words weren't all easily forthcoming, but he was clearly talking about how to get where he was going. "I think I have it figured out. What will everyone do? Is it OK? Tell me, what did we do in Connecticut?" He was sitting up and looking into my eyes with his own wide open. I hadn't seen the blues of his eyes since the summer, and I was so glad to see him and be seen by him. We studied each other for long happy minutes between the fragments of our words. I told him what a good dad he had been, how much love he had shared, and how he had lived a good and honest life. I told him how we used to play in the backyard and play word games by the fireplace in the living room and hide-and-seek throughout the house. I told him how much I loved him and assured him it was OK for him to go. He had done his work in the world and done it beautifully. His children and grandchildren were happy and healthy. I told him he had shown us all how to live with love, integrity, kindness, and honesty. I told him I trusted the process he was going through and encouraged him to trust too. I had said all of these things a few days earlier, but it was hard to tell how much he had absorbed. On this day, I know he heard me. He was so receptive and aware.

The chaplain arrived just as Dad and I were winding down our twenty-five-minute heart-to-heart exchange of conversational fragments, tears, hugs, and laughter. Dad was attentive and alert during the reading of the Sacrament of the Sick and the laying on of hands. Afterward, we all sat quietly for what felt like an hour but was probably only five minutes. I was crying streams of tears and broke the silence when I got up for a tissue. My movement inspired Dad to launch into more animated talking. His words were disjointed but clear. As he had before the chaplain arrived, he chatted excitedly, asking questions and reminiscing in bursts of words that didn't all connect. "All the people I will be seeing . . . I knew this time was coming. She'll be coming back for me. It is OK."

We listened and responded and joined him in affirmation that all was well. A while later, as the chaplain and I readied to leave, Dad said, "Thank you. When I woke up today, I knew I wanted to talk about all of this." Leaving Dad that day with words, hugs, chuckles, eye contact, and gratitude was so sweet and so hard. The chaplain said it was the first time Dad had looked at him in his month of visiting. I assured him it was more engagement than

I had seen in months and thanked him profusely. I was so grateful that receiving the Sacrament of the Sick had coincided with such a surprising and lucid afternoon. It felt as though Dad had come back from a deep and private place in order to say good-bye. I was so glad to be there and to be ready for the conversation he had wanted to have. I drove away wishing I had offered more or different words and that I had understood more of the meaning in his words. But I also drove away with a much lighter heart that afternoon and felt that Dad's heart was lightened too.

The next day when I went to visit, Dad was in his wheelchair. His usually fidgeting hands were calm on his lap, and he was wide awake and deep in distant thoughts. I said hello and gave him a kiss, and he replied with "Thank you, thank you." I sat quietly with him for a few minutes then told him I couldn't stay. I was on my way to the airport to pick up Thomas and Thatcher for Thanksgiving vacation. Thomas and I would be back in a few days to join him for Thanksgiving lunch. He replied with "Thank you, thank you." I answered, "Thank *you*," and stood to go. I was, in fact, incredibly grateful to see him so content and relaxed. The caregiver and I shared a glance and a smile. As she walked me to the door, she said, "He's been like this all morning." It was a huge shift. For weeks, he had been struggling with agitation, restlessness, and combativeness. Now, suddenly, he was at rest. Perhaps he could feel an opening in his body, the permission granted by our conversation, the forgiveness and promise granted by the Sacrament of the Sick, his own willingness and readiness to let go. It seemed that peace had found him, or maybe he had found peace.

It would be a month before he died. There were plenty of ups and downs yet to come, but at the time I was not thinking of the future or the past. I was simply grateful for this momentary deep breath of awareness and ease.

Staying Close

After Thanksgiving, Thomas and Thatcher returned to Dubai, Duncan went back to school, and I visited with Dad daily. He slept a lot, spending less time sitting up in the wheelchair and more and more time in bed. Eventually, Dad kept his eyes closed and sank so deeply into himself he seemed mostly unaware of the physical world around him. Sometimes he would respond to music or my voice with a change in facial expression or a lifted hand. Sometimes he seemed to be responding to an inner dialogue that provided comfort and guidance. On those days, he would smile, clap his hands, and reach out as if to gently touch something. I was honored to bear witness, but if I felt restless by his side, I would not stay with him for long. Instead, I walked the beaches we had often visited together over the last three years. I tried to will the expansiveness of the sky and sea into the quiet, dark room where he lay. I wrote letters to him when I got home.

Dear Dad,

You are lying alone, dying. Yet I sense you are not alone. I know that there are many people loving you, thinking of you, and wishing you transcendence from your situation. Our energy is with you even when our bodies are not, but I struggle to be sure that is enough. Surely you are doing work that is yours alone to accomplish. Sometimes when I am by your bedside, I am afraid to move lest my movement disturb your focus. You are inward.

I feel called to think of your full self, when you were out in the world, living a life of intention and care. You worked hard to provide for others, to live a just and honest life, and to secure a future that was full of hope and security. You succeeded by leaps and bounds. Yet you lie here alone. Could this be OK? It seems the world should offer you more. But you would never complain. Why should I? It is not my place. By your example, I have learned that humility and integrity are virtues to live each day. Selflessness is its own reward and a life of generosity is a life well-lived. You were not "saving for a rainy day" or delaying gratification for the future, you were living as you wished, in service to others. I couldn't be more grateful and honored to be responsible for carrying forward that legacy.

As you lie dying and I am sitting here crying, I wish you a full awareness that your life was meaningful and powerful. I will carry your lessons always, and I will honor your whole life, the exploratory youth, dedicated studiousness, earnest marriage, juggling parenting, lonely empty-nesting, and challenging aging. You carried each stage with grace. I wish I could have seen and helped sooner, but my *could haves* are pointless. In fact, you didn't need them either, further testament to your strength and integrity. I have learned so much in the last few years as I have moved in closer to "help." I have gained as much as I have given, that's for sure. Perhaps that is always the case. In our giving, we are fulfilled. For that truly may be what we are meant to do in this life. If that is the case, you have done it well.

As you lie dying, we need only celebrate the completion of a life well-lived and recommit ourselves to carrying forward all that we have learned from you.

With love and gratitude,

Lisa

When I was by Dad's bedside and when I left him, I practiced stillness and deep listening. I had learned to be quiet in our togetherness on the park bench while we watched the waves, and now I transferred that teaching to a meditation cushion by his side. I could just be present with him, as he was in each moment. Even when I was not with him, I found myself keeping vigil and staying with him in my thoughts and intentions. At home in the evenings, I listened to Dad's favorite songs and continued to direct my attention and energy to him. I kept a rock from the beach in my pocket during the day and slept with it on my chest at night, a reminder to my own spirit to remain with my body and the earth while I visualized Dad's spirit unraveling from its earthly restrictions.

Subject: Dad needs your energy and love

Hi All,

Please send Dad extra love and strength for his journey tonight. He is working hard and needs our love and support.

Dad has been throwing up and in bed today . . .
I stayed with him for several hours and he was very out of it, uncomfortable and restless. He eventually settled into a restful sleep. I left to take a walk and came back 1.5 hours later to find him still deeply asleep. The furrow had left his brow, which tells me he was truly relaxed and comfortable.

I will call Rosen Springs first thing in the morning to get an update and will let you know what I hear. I will go down again by midmorning if not sooner. Regardless of what else is happening in his body, rehydrating after a day without liquid will be tricky. If you have questions or want more info, please let me know. I am less sure than ever how much detail is useful. It seems the most important thing right now is to send our love and energy to Dad and trust that he will use it as he needs.

Wishing you all love and sending all of our collective energy and love to Dad.

Four days before Dad died, I felt the beginning of his final letting go. As I drove south to be with him, tangled as always in my thoughts of him, I was suddenly filled with an overwhelming certainty that peace had settled. It felt like Dad was already released from his body in some way and, though I was not physically with him, I was still with him. Or maybe he was now with me. In that moment I understood that the universe is vast enough to hold past, present, and future at once. It is expansive enough to hold mind, body, and spirit and capacious enough to hold you, me, and everyone who is, was, and will be. I was graced with an indescribable feeling and awareness of the infinite. This intuition settled into me as truth. It was not something I could see, touch, or prove. I can still barely find words to describe it, but I knew it.

Thirty minutes later, the earth confirmed my new understanding. I turned a corner on the highway and was in a winter wonderland. Water had evaporated from the bay during the sunny afternoon the day before, and the moisture in the air had come to rest on the trees along the highway overnight. As temperatures fell, the water froze and ice coated the needles on each branch of every tree. They glistened and sparkled, reflecting the morning sun brilliantly. Heaven, earth, and sea had merged. As I caught my breath and remembered to pay attention to the road, a flock of birds rose up in unison. They formed a circle, collapsed into the center of that form, and dove.

They rose again in a spiral and flew out of sight. There were dozens of cars on the highway and I hoped others had seen the magnificent sights, but I knew these glorious displays of life and beauty were messages for me.

Seconds later my phone rang. It was Rosen Springs. Dad's breathing had changed. They had already called hospice and thought I should come down. I let them know I was already almost there. I hadn't needed the phone call. I had been receiving messages the whole drive. Dad's spirit was well on its way; his body would have to pass soon too. All was well.

Letting Go

My brothers came and we settled in to keep Dad company. We were there to bear witness to his dying, hoping that he felt surrounded by love and assured by our words and presence. All four of his children were there. His work was done. He had raised us to be conscientious, responsible adults, and we were now raising our children in that same effort. Our presence confirmed we had come to live the same values that Dad embodied: hard work, patience, persistence, honesty, goodness, and kindness. The chaplain came and read the Last Rites while my brothers and I laid our hands on my Dad. The hospice nurse told us "it won't be long now." His breathing became slower and shallower. For a whole afternoon, we counted five shallow breaths in a row and waited ten, then twenty, then thirty seconds before another series would begin. The Rosen Springs medication nurse came in every four hours, then every two, and finally every hour to provide him with the pain medication that kept him from gasping for air and wincing with the struggle. The care staff came twice a day to bathe him and put on a clean shirt. They tended to his body with the same loving care with which my brothers and I hoped to tend to his heart.

The days and nights the five of us spent in that room merged together. We alternated between talking and silence. We talked about our kids, our jobs, our spouses. We reminisced about other family members and meaningful moments of compassion and grace that Dad had offered us as we had grown up. We listened to his favorite songs and Christmas carols playing on repeat. We took turns holding Dad's hands and gently rubbing his shoulders. We told him over and over again how much we loved him and thanked him for the life and values he had given us. The staff began to encourage us to get out for a while, explaining that many parents won't die in front of their children, protecting them even as they are passing on. That seemed likely for Dad, who had always carried his burdens stoically, alone and out of sight. We tried to balance the desire to be with Dad with the desire to give him space. We created opportunities to leave the room and said good-bye, as if for the last time, each time we left. We lingered over lunch and dinner. We took long walks and drives. After three days, Willy and Matthew both said final good-byes and went home to their families with tears in their eyes. Thomas arrived and sat with Dad for a few minutes, assuring him that he would take care of me, thanking him for the guidance, love, and encouragement he had given us as a couple and as individuals. We went to dinner as the staff came in to clean Dad up for the night. As we walked past the window outside, we could see the two young caregivers shaving his thin cheeks and narrow chin.

When Peter and I got back from dinner, Dad was breathing steadily, and I suddenly realized I had been clinging to his dying just as I had previously clung to his living. I did not know what would replace this dying vigil or the caregiving relationship we had shared. And so I had hung on, even as he lay dying. I worried I had made it hard for him to die because I was still holding on to his life so tightly. Life is all that we know; letting go of it was clearly hard work for me too. For years his life had been only the present moment. Aspiration, regret, fear, and longing were my projections, not his realities. I had been practicing being in the moment with him for months, letting each one go as a new one arose. It was time to really embrace that teaching. As I said good night, I said goodbye for real and assured him I was truly ready. I was. As the evening wore on and Peter and I settled into sleep, we heard his breathing getting quieter, shallower, and slower.

Dad died with the same gentle strength he had lived with, slowly and quietly. He slipped away in the still dark of early morning while Peter and I were sleeping just a few feet away. It was very like him to wait until we were not looking and exit quietly.

Dad's body was washed and dressed one final time. Peter and I lingered for a while, waiting for the funeral home to come, but a snowstorm was approaching and we realized there really was nothing for us to do. In the hallway, we could hear care staff and residents beginning to prepare for the day. It was time for us to leave. When we stepped into the still, dark morning, fresh snow falling, I took a deep breath. The world was the same. It seemed implausible. I had just felt it crumbling. Yet here was familiarity. The air was crisp. The sun would be rising soon. Peter wrapped his arm around me and walked me to the car. I could not understand how or why, but I knew that my heart, mind, and body had experienced something wholly new and all mine yet also completely universal.

❧ 5 ❧

Reemergence

Honoring the Wilderness and the Journey Ahead

When we leave the trail at the end of a long hike, Thomas and I have a ritual. As we step off the trail at the trailhead, we turn back toward it. With hands together, we bow and offer our thanks. We give thanks to the trail. We give thanks to each other and to the earth for the journey we have had. In that moment of gratitude, we also set an intention to carry the lessons from the trail into our lives.

Shifting Sands

The ground beneath my feet seemed to tremble with aftershocks for months after my Dad died. It was as if a hole had opened in the universe and I was waiting for the molecules around me to shift into place and create a new order. I thought I had mourned Dad's passing years earlier when dementia interrupted our father-daughter relationship and nudged me into caregiving. I thought I had done a pretty thorough job of grieving and longing for the life we could no longer share together. When he physically died, I realized there was even more sadness and grief to release. The little girl I had been still longed for the father who steadied, nurtured, and advised. The caregiver I had become longed to feel needed, valued, helpful. In losing my Dad, I had lost two pieces of my identity. My missing roles created cracks in my self-concept and my self-confidence. I kept asking, *Now what?* An empty chasm existed where once there had been mutual care and love and commitment. But each new moment that arose continued to demand my attention, and eventually I accepted these new fissures as beautiful and powerful imperfections. They are evidence of *my* life well-lived and will remain central aspects of my being for the rest of my days. They give me an appreciation of life and work that shifted my perspective, heightened my awareness, and now guides my intentional action. Both caregiving and grieving are now a part of the history that will inform my future.

In the feeling of overwhelming loss right after Dad died, there was something reminiscent of the days after my first son was born. My labor with Duncan was long and hard. I had wanted a natural childbirth, but at fourteen days past due, I was admitted to the maternity ward and labor was induced by a chemical wrapped around my cervix to soften it. After several hours of long, hard contractions, I called a friend who had given birth to her first child a year before. I was panicking, certain that I could not do it. She assured me I could. Not only that, she confided, the only way out of labor was to go through it to the other side. Her reassurance was calming and practical. Of course, she was right. Two long days and nights later, Duncan was born. He was perfect, beautiful, and vociferous. Labor and birth had been hard on him too.

A day later when the hospital staff told us it was time to go home, we were not ready. We wanted to stay where we would be assured we were doing a good job and Duncan was healthy and growing. Surely we couldn't be on our own. Panic set in again. We didn't know how to parent yet. They couldn't possibly send us home with this innocent, helpless baby. We had grown accustomed to the support of the hospital nurses during the long labor. But they told us we would be fine, checked the fit of his car seat, and nudged us out the door. When we got home, I remember feeling like it would be impossible to return to the world we had known. I can still remember the quality of light when we walked into our house. Though it was midday, the light was dim and a haze made it feel as though there was a veil over my eyes. It could have been my exhaustion, but I felt like I was literally filtering the world through a new perspective. With childbirth and the almost crippling responsibility of caring for a new life, we had entered a new dimension. I was filled with awe in my newfound awareness of what all the parents in the world had been through. I was humbled to have joined their ranks, and both nervous and overjoyed about the possibilities that lay ahead of us.

I recognize that now as the feeling of touching life's edges and nearly reaching beyond. As with the process of birth, moving through the process of death is an inevitable part of life. At both birth and death, we touch the far ends of the continuum that remind us life is like a flowing river. Both life and rivers share a beginning, a meandering middle, and an end. But the river is simply one element in the water cycle, a place of containment that has its start and end points within a never-ending circle. Attending a birth or a death, we get a glimpse beyond the edges to a realm where the cycle of life continues. It is powerful and humbling to bear witness to another being's passage into or out of life, and it is a sharp reminder that our own life is both finite and infinite too. When I consider my Dad's continuum, I reclaim and relive the lessons of his life and especially the last years we spent together in a new way. I can sense his essence welling up in me, and I see it lived in the world around me. His strong values of honesty and goodness, kindness and compassion live on. In his time on the earth, he personified and amplified these values. It is my turn to ensure that I am doing the same.

Afterthought

Caring for, loving, and grieving for my Dad has heightened my resolve to live a life of intention and meaning. The lessons I learned during these years were familiar. I had seen many of them before but did not recognize them because the circumstances were so different. My experience of searching, growing, and learning in relationship to the land, to others, and finally to myself has repeated on a seemingly endless spiral. But, of course, it will have an ending just as it had a beginning. Now that I have touched on a new awareness of beginnings and endings with my heart and body, my story may evolve. I will know in time, and I am prepared to greet a new path if and when it arises. For now, though, I embrace the familiar values of my landscape with renewed enthusiasm.

Once I recognized it fully, caregiving for Dad was valuable, meaningful work for me and for our family. My years in service to him were joyful, heart-wrenching, uplifting, challenging, and deeply satisfying. As Gandhi once said, "The best way to find yourself is in service to others." I did find myself during the years of my Dad's journey with dementia. I was simply there, doing what mattered. I now realize that is what I have always done and it is what I must continue to do with intention. Now that Dad has died and my children are growing up, I am aware of a spaciousness created by my expanded generosity. Without careful attention, it would be easy to fall back into proceeding through life as if contributions to the economy are more important than contributions to family and society. I have seen, though, that there is nothing more important than simply showing up for one another, giving and receiving with care, love, and attention. As in the past, I will remain ready to respond to needs and opportunities as they arise, but I also feel compelled to take the next path with careful attention. I no longer expect or hope for a map. I am prepared to move forward one step at a time, trusting in the process and living deeply into each moment as it comes and as it goes.

Acknowledgments

In caregiving, wilderness living, parenting, and writing this book, Thomas has been a constant source of inspiration and encouragement. I am forever grateful for his company on this amazing journey that is our life together.

With enduring love, I give thanks to my dad who, unwittingly, entered uncharted territory and allowed me to come along. For these intense years together, I am honored. At first, I hesitated to expose so much of this private man's struggle. Ultimately, I believe that he would welcome this telling and join me in the hope that this book may offer light, company, and courage to other families facing the unknown.

About the Author

After growing up in small towns of New England and Wisconsin, Lisa Steele-Maley developed a strong connection to the affirming rhythms of the wilderness while working in the mountains and coasts of Alaska and Washington State. She seeks opportunities to help individuals and organizations cultivate healthy, responsible relationships within their communities and with the earth. Lisa lives in an aging farmhouse on the coast of Maine with her husband, two teenage sons, and a handful of animals.

616 STEE
Steele-Maley, Lisa.
Without a map:

JUL 3 0 2018

CPSIA information can be obtained
at www.ICGtesting.com
Printed in the USA
LVHW04s1729030718
582629LV00001B/138/P

9 781618 521224